FLOWERS FOR SALE

Growing and Marketing Cut Flowers

Backyard to Small Acreage

by Lee Sturdivant

Illustrations by Peggy Sue McRae

A Bootstrap *Guide*

Published by San Juan Naturals
Friday Harbor, Washington

Published by
SAN JUAN NATURALS
P.O. Box 642
Friday Harbor, Washington 98250

Book Design by Words & Deeds, San Jose

Printed in the United States of America

ISBN #0-9621635-1-1

Library of Congress Catalogue Card No. 91-67892

10   9   8   7   6   5   4   3   2

SECOND PRINTING, SEPTEMBER 1992

For Brian and Molly

ACKNOWLEDGMENTS

Many sources and authorities were helpful in writing this book, and many of those are cited in the bibliography.

My special acknowledgment and thanks go to the busy people, both growers and flower sellers, who so graciously took time from their lives to allow me to interview them for this book. Thanks again to Graham Baldree, Susan Bill, Bill Carli, Fanny and George Carroll, Frances and John Chadwick, Dave Clark, Gary Franco, Annely Germaine, Vicki Giannangelo, Nancy and Dennis Grandee, Rick Kaminskis, Vince Law, Don Moran, Mary Karen Ryan, Al and Genevieve Schultz, Paul and Alison Kutz Troutman, and Lesa Waldron.

Other helpful people I would like to thank include: Pat Brash, Lee Campbell, John Dustrude, Louise Dustrude, Martha Kaye, Judy Laushman, Suzette Mahr, Peggy Sue McRae, and Tal Sturdivant.

CONTENTS

ꕔ Appendix

FIRST BOUQUETS

WELCOME TO
THE GARDEN

I live on a 120' by 180' town lot in Friday Harbor, Washington, where I have been growing fruits and vegetables for my family, plus culinary herbs, and lots of flowers for cutting. I started a cut flower business from that garden a few years ago and on a typical day in late June, I could walk out and cut for selling at my local market and to private customers:

20 blue delphiniums.............................$ 20.00

10 mixed bouquets 40.00

40 stems of Sweet William 7.00

2 wedding bouquets 35.00

That's over a hundred dollars worth of flowers in a day, from a relatively small garden full of plants that will keep on producing even more flowers. Most of the plants I've just picked from will produce more blossoms for sale in only a few more days.

Fresh garden flowers are a seemingly ordinary product of so many backyards all around us, yet they can have a far greater monetary value than you might imagine.

They are one of the most valuable things you can grow on your property—far more valuable, I found, than almost any fruit or vegetable you might choose to grow and sell.

Cut flower sales in this country are definitely on the upswing with big increases predicted for the future. What should interest a small or backyard grower of cut flowers in these predictions is that the big interest is coming in old fashioned garden flowers—like those your mother or grandmother grew. Like the ones you are probably growing right now. If you are interested in a small, home-based business, cut flower growing is definitely worth your consideration.

Over the past few years I have been earning my money (not a tremendous amount—never more than $22,000 per year) in various part-time enterprises: growing and selling culinary herbs; growing and selling cut flowers; some writing and publishing; and a two day a week, eight dollar per hour job as a ferry dock attendant. During those years, I have also tried my hand at a U-Pick berry field, keeping bees for honey, and growing potted plants for sale.

This book is a recounting of the flower business part of those years, and the flower business knowledge I have been able to collect from others in putting together this book. Some of the information is based on a series of interviews with small growers in three states, plus conversations with florists, flower brokers, and wholesale buyers, county agents, and grower's organizations—everyone, in fact, who could shed a little light on this seldom written about subject—the cut flower business and how to transplant yourself into it.

The first part of the book tells of my own limited flower sales experience—as a bouquet seller in my local supermarket for three years. I give a lot of details on how to do this and would recommend it to anyone as an easy to start, easy to do, fun business. It can earn you some good money in the flower season and make your own garden offer something more than the hard work and great joy you've always gotten from it.

I give some general information on harvesting and conditioning of flowers so that you can make whatever it is you're growing (or harvesting from the wild) last as long as possible. There are hints on arrangement and presentation, on dealing with retail sales outlets, and a few business details to help you get started.

Then I step out to take a look at other small growers and find some interesting possibilities that may be applicable in your own situation. I visited quite a variety of growers—from those who grow and sell tiny stephanotis blossoms to those who sell flowers from fruit trees; from those who sell at Saturday markets and U Pick farms to those who deal with large wholesale houses in their area.

There are interviews with several flower buyers—from one who buys small amounts of flower blossoms for his calligraphy pictures, to an international broker who deals with over eighty growers in the U.S. and Mexico.

I also attended flower auctions in Canada, Southern California and Holland (where I also did a lot of bicycle riding!) and learned about this exciting way that some flower growers have joined together to form huge cooperative flower auctions for retail customers.

Toward the end of the book are long lists of flowers: perennials, annuals, biennials, bulbs, shrubs, even trees, vines and herbs, that are the very best for growers of cut flowers. I give some basic information on many of them, from culture and propagation to specific harvest and conditioning information on many species. Even if you never grow for marketing—using your garden flowers only as gifts and for your own pleasure—you will likely find the listings of plants to be very helpful in growing the right plants for cutting.

At the end of the book, I offer other reference material so that no matter where you live, you can find what you need in the way of seeds, plants, supplies, and more information to turn your flower garden or small acreage into something more financially productive.

This is a book about learning to earn money from growing flowers but, in my mind, it also exists in a little larger context that deserves a brief mention.

In this time of mega and multinational corporations, workaholism, and the acquisition of great wealth, I am drawn more and more to small, independent, home-based businesses; to part-time and spare-time work, and a simpler, more modest life. I often suspect that my hankering toward the small, simple and spare may just be a reaction and adaptation to a new world-wide, far more competitive economy that seems to be overtaking us. I look "out there" and the world looks much tougher to work in these days; the pace is ever faster, the demands ever greater. I take a walk in my flower garden and the world falls back into order again. Like many others, I believe that when the world really wears us out, the garden is the place to be.

A FLOWERY
IDEA

It's a July morning in my town as I write this. At the local Saturday farmers' market, several people are selling bunches of flowers in recycled mayonnaise jars for two or three dollars per bunch. Two blocks away a flower shop has floral bouquets and arrangements displayed in their cooler at fifteen to thirty-five dollars apiece.

Some of the the florist bouquets have a cellophane paper wrapper, a more formal look about them, with bits of greenery included. They have fewer flowers than the colorful bunches at the farmers' market, but the market flowers are tied with a rubber band, have relatively short stems (all of the same length), and are sitting in the summer sunshine looking far more fragile than the florist bouquets.

This big gap in price and presentation drew my friend Pat Brash and me to try our hands at selling bouquets at our local supermarket. What if, we wondered, one could show "arranged" bouquets with lots of greenery in the supermarket , and sell the bouquets from, say, four to ten dollars each? How much would the market take from that sale? What if the flowers didn't sell? How and where would they be displayed? We'd definitely have to get some answers to these questions before we did anything else.

The second thing that drew us to flower sales was a deep love of flower growing along with an awareness of the increasing cost of pursuing that hobby. Each year the cost of everything to do with gardening is going up— sometimes dramatically.

When I first began gardening rather seriously, we paid a small flat fee for water use. Now it costs by the gallon and the costs go up at least once a year. Seed packets only a few years ago were less than fifty cents per packet. Now it's not uncommon to have to pay over three dollars for anything unusual—and the packets have fewer seeds than they did before. Garden tools and supplies are a real investment now; a decent shovel or rake that looks like it could, with care, last a few years, now costs up to forty dollars or more.

In other words, gardening is no longer the low cost hobby it was once considered. If you take your gardening seriously, your costs are going up and up. So selling some of what you grow just makes good sense.

FIRST STEPS
TAKEN

There are six steps to follow to set up and operate a small floral bouquet business (as I did). The first part of this book is about these six steps:

Step #1. Find a place to sell your flowers and get the display and billing details settled.

Step #2. Establish a small business, including some simple billing procedures.

Step #3. Harvest, condition and arrange flowers.

Step #4. Deliver bouquets to the store.

Step #5. Check back to see how the flowers are doing.

Step #6. Pick up any rejects.

Start over with Step #3 again.

When we decided to try flower selling, I had already been selling fresh culinary herbs to my local supermarkets (see *Profits From Your Backyard Herb Garden*[1]). So I had good relationships with the managers there and could easily go in to talk with them about flowers. Their flower sales at that time only amounted to a few daffodils in early spring, flowers grown by a local bulb grower.

Their primary concerns were about space and waste, so those had to become our concerns, too. I already had an arrangement in the case of my herbs, to take back any that didn't sell (and thus control the quality of the displays). Pat and I decided that we were willing to offer the same deal on flower bouquets and that made the store managers immediately interested in talking further about flower sales. Market people are much more interested in trying new ideas if they know that any first losses on anything new will not have to be borne by them.

Chances are you don't already have a selling arrangement at your market, so that is the first thing you must do: choose a retail outlet you think will be the best place to sell your flowers. It does not have to be a market. Flowers can be sold in drug stores, gift shops, garden centers, variety stores, even little convenience stores. The important thing is that the location have a **high traffic volume**: many people going through the store who will see your flowers.

Once you've decided where they should go, then you have to find out what's a good time to speak to the manager and tell him or her what you have in mind. If you can possibly take and show a bouquet or two, that would be even better. Just remember these are very busy people, so figure out exactly what you want to get across before you go into the meeting. Be brief, friendly, and cooperative:

"I grow these lovely flowers and think we can both make some money if you let me sell them here. I will bring them in all arranged, put them in containers near the cash registers, and check them every day or so to take out any that don't look perfect. I will set the prices and you will earn 30% of the retail price. I will take the loss on any that don't sell."

That's the message you want to get across. If you should get turned down, try another location. After you've had some success in selling at one place, it is much easier to go back to the first place and try again. Your confidence will have increased—you'll know much more about what you have to offer. It's just getting your toe in the door that first time that can seem a little intimidating. Remember that buyers for stores do just that all the time: they buy, buy, buy. Your floral idea is just one more thing they have to consider. If they haven't tried selling flowers, it's something they should try as more and more markets and stores around the country are doing so. And you can offer them an easy, no-risk way to try it.

The space problem in our market turned out to be a bit trickier than getting a first O.K. to try flower selling there. First of all, we listened to the manager's concerns about the crowded space near the cash registers, which we knew to be the very best spot for flowers (and almost anything else), and then we made a trip to a florist supply house and purchased a few black plastic cone-shaped containers. These fit into metal holders that could be screwed onto the wooden partitions separating the check stands. The manager was wary about these but willing to try them for a start. He approved the idea tentatively and we then brought up some other details. We asked if he would be willing to let us set the prices on the bouquets and pass on to the store thirty percent of the retail price for whatever sold. He agreed to that and we were off and picking.

The hanging containers were fine for about three weeks (of very good sales) and one of us went in there to

Cone and holder

check on things and, lo and behold, the cones had been taken away from the check stands and placed in the produce section. What's more, the flower bouquets had stopped selling. Yikes! We were really shocked, found the manager and then we all told each other our problems. His problem was that one of the checkers was allergic to flowers, and he thought it was a little too crowded up there by the check stand, anyway. Our problem was that the flowers, after three weeks of excellent sales, simply weren't selling from the fruit and vegetable department. Once we pointed that out to him, he thought we all had to come up with another solution. His primary concern turned out to be exactly the one we had: sales volume. But he certainly preferred the sales success coming without too many extra problems to handle—like an employee who was allergic to blossoms.

We found the girl with the allergy problem and she said she thought the flowers were great but they just couldn't be that close to her nose. The other checkers came around to listen and one of them made a suggestion: "Why not put them all in big pots or buckets on this last check stand down here—the one we only use when we are super busy—and we can work around them there if we have to. People really love these flowers," she said, "and that way we can keep them and everyone will be happy." The allergic clerk nodded. She also liked having lovely bouquets nearby—just not **that** nearby. From that day on, we put our flowers in plastic buckets on that one check stand (where every customer who walked in the door passed closely by them), and our sales immediately jumped up again.

I am convinced that customers prefer to pick up their bouquets just before they leave the store, so that they don't have to carry them in their cart, dripping water, and worry that they will start to wilt. The further the flowers are from the cash register and front doors of a store, the less bouquets will sell. So just keep trying to get to that position.

⚘

One interesting aside to this is that Pat Brash was so into flowers and flower growing that a couple of years later she ended up purchasing a local flower shop—which she still owns and runs quite successfully. We often laugh together now about our intense involvement that first year of flower sales to the local supermarket. We called our business, "Bloomers". And though we've both gone on to other things, our gardening friends still sell flowers in that same supermarket. And the market itself now has a real flower department which they keep stocked from local growers and from larger, more commercial suppliers. But that's jumping ahead of the story a bit.

One of the first questions you might be asking is, "How much do I have to grow to be able to do a bouquet business. How many plants, how many flowers?" The quick answer is: as much as you like. But a more accurate answer is: as much as you can. In my own experience at growing and in the experience of others I've talked to, there is almost never a question of growing too much if you stay at all active in selling.

As I said at the beginning, I don't have a very big yard and I do a lot of other growing, but I put cut flowers into every spare inch of growing space I thought I could spare for it. I still got orders all the time from people wanting flowers for weddings or flowers for parties that I simply couldn't fill.

Once the word gets around that you are growing flowers for sale, you will be called repeatedly by people needing flowers for this or that occasion. Of course, the calls don't always come at the right time—when you have extra ones to sell. But my point is that you won't waste many flowers once you get into the business and start selling. In fact, you'll miss all the blooms you usually have in your yard. Every time it gets full of blossoms, you'll be out there cutting them all off, and then waiting for them to grow back so you can cut some more.

---

[1] See the order section in the back of the book.

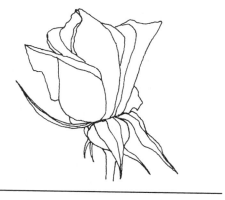

DETAILS, DETAILS, DETAILS

Pat and I weren't sure just how to run a partnership in this venture because we both had flower gardens, but starting out together probably gave us the courage to take the first steps in something we hadn't done before. We found out almost immediately that what we had were two separate businesses and that whatever flowers either one of us would take in to that market would sell. In fact, neither of us realized just how many flowers could be sold in that way, and we were kept very, very busy that first season just trying to keep up with that pleasant news.

Soon it was just more convenient for each of us to be in the flower selling business to the same store. We would take turns taking bouquets in and would pick up any of our bunches that didn't sell. The weekends were so busy that we found we could both take flowers in for the weekend and both batches would usually sell. We ended up each billing the store at the end of each two week period and each getting checks in the mail for what we had done.

Our first purchase, after getting a go-ahead from our market, was a rubber stamp. In this country, it's usually just that one little step that can put anyone in business. Choose a name and buy a rubber stamp with the business name, address, and telephone number on it: usually your home address (or wherever you receive mail) and your phone number. It's amazing, really, but that is truly all it takes to get started.

The only major piece of equipment we felt we needed for the flower sale business was a refrigerator to store the cut flowers in before taking them to market. I have since known flower growers who do a lot of business without refrigeration, but Pat and I both found it very, very helpful to have an old refrigerator in which we stored nothing but flowers during the selling season. The ethylene gas from fruits and vegetables can *ripen* the flowers too fast, so it's best to keep flowers by themselves in coolers.

This is also a good time to mention something I intend to show all through this book, and that is that there are so many ways to approach this flower selling business that no one can ever say they know the best or only way to do it. I have met many flower growers who do so many things just the opposite of the last grower I talked to, and yet everyone is selling flowers.

I have friends now who sell bouquets in markets without any greenery whatsoever. I always did mine with lots of greenery. I thought I needed a refrigerator, yet I have met quite large growers who never have felt they needed one. Some people use flower preservative, others think it a waste of money.

So in reading these details of the way I sold bouquets to my local market, please remember that you are free to embellish or simplify in any way you choose and chances are, if you've chosen the right place to sell your bouquets, and you grow lots of flowers, you will do just fine. I may give details as though they are the only possible way to do things but they most certainly are not.

Now let's move ahead to that happy day when you have a "go ahead and try" from a nearby merchant and a garden full of flowers ready to pick. Soon you are going to cut, condition, and arrange the flowers for market. But when you take them into the store to sell, you'll need an invoice book with you so that someone can sign for the flowers. This is proof of delivery and it also helps you keep track of what you have sold. More importantly, it allows you to collect your money.

Invoice books are for sale inexpensively in any office supply store, in many drug stores, variety stores, etc. You probably need a book of duplicate (rather than triplicate) forms and they come with or without carbon. Use your rubber stamp at the top of the first copy of each invoice and that's all you need to do the billing to your store. The important thing to remember is to have someone sign the invoice each time you take flowers in.

You can use a new invoice for each delivery, but it is more economical to do several deliveries to the same store on a single invoice and turn it in at the end of each week or two week period. Just have someone sign each time you deliver. At the end of the invoice period, add up what you have taken in, subtract any that are rejects and then subtract the 30% that belongs to the store. The remaining total is what the store owes you.

I usually show my **terms** on the invoice as **net 10 days,** meaning I wish to be paid the full amount (no discounts) in ten days from the day I give the bill. Actually, some markets will even pay you cash as soon as you present the bill, but always collect what's owed to you before you let much build up in new deliveries. You're too small an operator to be giving much credit to anyone.

As a bouquet seller to stores you are a flower whole-saler, so you don't need to charge any sales tax. The store charges sales taxes in states and counties that have such taxes Sales taxes are charged only at the retail level.

Your town or county may charge a small business license fee. My town charges me $42 per year for the privilege of doing business here—using the town streets, I suppose, to take my flowers to market.

At the end of the year, of course, I must declare my income and expenses for the flower business and show those on our regular tax return.

Incidentally, it is immediately obvious that any garden growing business can have a pretty big expense bill with it—gardens are expensive whether you are selling flowers from them or not. That expense "write off" may also be one of the big advantages of a successful flower selling business. But the invoicing is the only new book-keeping necessary in this business. Keep your invoicing correct and up to date and, by the end of the year, you'll have a perfectly adequate record of what you've sold and earned.

When I first started a home based business, I kept track of business expenses in my regular checkbook by marking each entry with a big star for anything that should be declared as a business expense.That way I could easily separate these out at the end of the year when it was time to add up everything. Nowadays I have a separate bank account for business only, but there's no real need of this in the very beginning. Just keep clear notes in your checkbooks, on your checks themselves and, of course, receipts for anything of any value that you purchase. Once you are selling from your own garden, every expense for that garden becomes a business expense.

Before we get to the section on harvest and conditioning of your flowers, I want to tell you about an uncommon aspect of my cut flower business that I thought made it all more than worthwhile.

COLLECTING
FROM THE WILD

I'm convinced that one of the things that made my flower business such a success is that, from the beginning, I included greens and flowers from the wild in my bouquets. The wild stuff is what's growing out there in the country all around us and that many people never seem to notice, or else they label everything wild as "weeds." Take a walk in your neighborhood or in the countryside nearby and start to notice what grows naturally in your area. It can make your bouquets into something very special and unusual. Whether any such specific material is appropriate for your bouquets or will hold up along with the flowers is a subject we'll handle in the section on harvesting and conditioning. For the moment, start to notice the wild stuff. Your flower customers will love you for it.

I used the leathery leaves of salal (resembling lemon leaves) for greenery, along with sword ferns which also grow so plentifully in our area. I also used mullein, wild onions, several different sedges and rushes, cattails, wild grasses, plus many different kinds of tree branches, and countless stems of unusual plants I found in the vacant lots, woods, and along roadsides near my home. Some I could identify as saxifrages, wild legumes, even wild lupine that grow nearby—some I never could identify and am still trying to find out what they are.

If you do decide to collect flowers and greens from the wild, there are several considerations I'd like to mention. Foremost is the environmental concern. A mob of people going out after wild stuff across the land can be pretty damaging unless they really know what they are doing.

So the first rule is: **find out what you're doing**. Get some books from the library on what grows wild in your region and learn to identify the plants you are interested in. Find out if they are poisonous, if they are an endangered species. A good place to start for this information is the botany department of the closest university, or the county agent of your area. Both can tell you which reference books will apply in your region.

My favorite part of the bouquet business very quickly became this search for the wild stuff to add to my bouquets. I like nothing better than spending time out of doors learning about the plants that grow all around us. Adding these finds to your week's bouquets makes them very special; flower buyers love buying a bouquet with unusual plants tucked into it.

The second thing of importance to remember is not to take too much of anything from the wild. Unless you know for certain that a field or lot is going to be developed right away, always leave plenty of material growing so that it will be there for the next season, and for the next passerby. We are losing countless species of plants and animals these days. It's important that we all take special care not to contribute to that loss in our gathering from the wild.

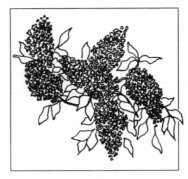

Lilac

But if you like to wander in fields and forests as I do, you can come across wondrous finds that you can add to your bouquets. Hawthorn and *Amelanchier* branches in early spring are truly fabulous just as they come into blossom. You can sell these as bouquets even without adding flowers.

Rushes or sedges add a perfect uncommon touch to a bouquet of purple monkshood and bright orange calendulas. "Rushes are round and sedges have edges," goes the old saying to help you identify your finds.

I even know of old homesteads where purple lilac bushes grow to twenty feet and arching stems of spirea bloom profusely, with no one there to pick the flowers. Except for me.

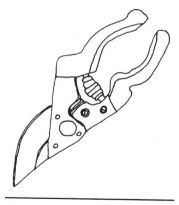

HARVEST AND CONDITIONING

Some general comments on harvesting and conditioning are next, but remember that the Cut Flower Catalog section of this book also contains information about the harvest and conditioning of many specific flowers.

Twenty years or so ago, the harvest and conditioning of flowers consisted almost solely of cutting flowers when they seemed mature and putting them in water so that they would last a few days. Since that time, science and technology have brought big changes in the flower world (just as in every other part of our world). And now it is possible to cut carnations in South America (where so many of them are grown) and, through special handling that includes the use of strong chemicals and the latest in storage techniques, to hold those already cut carnations for up to six months (!) before sending them to market as fresh cut flowers.

The use of chemicals in the treatment of commercial cut flowers is so widespread in Europe now, that many types of cut flowers taken to auction in Aalsmeer, Holland (the largest flower auction in the world) must be pre-treated with silver thiosulphate solution or some other powerful floral preservative. Samples of each lot of flowers brought to auction are tested and if they are found to be untreated, the whole lot is discarded and cannot be sold. This heavy use of chemicals is an effort to keep fresh flower holding standards high. It has also led to such bizarre results as the six month old 'fresh cut' carnations.

The post harvest handling is not the only thing that determines the life of flowers after cutting. Tests have shown that too much nitrogen fertilizer, for instance, can create large lush flowers that fade very rapidly once cut. Light intensity affects the sugar content of flowers and thus their storage life. Water and humidity are also important, as are air pollution, temperature, and sanitation. Another of the more important things that can cause early ripening or spoilage of cut flowers is the presence of ethylene gas: it speeds up the maturation of the flowers and causes spoilage.

Many if not most of the cut flowers now shipped daily around the world by air are kept out of water and then re-hydrated at their destinations. Much of the chemical use is to help the flowers take up the water they have been deprived of during the dry, cold storage used in shipping. There are also special chemical solutions to help flower buds open after harvest and to hold off the effects of ethylene gas and bacteria.

I find all of this information about the latest methods of after-harvest handling of flowers very interesting, but it only seems to be of real importance when flowers are being shipped and handled over long times and distances. For the kinds of flower sales we are talking about in a bouquet garden—and in the sales by all the other flower growers I met with in the writing of this book— only a few simple steps are necessary. The very freshness that comes with small growing efforts done close to the market keeps everything easy and straightforward. Only the simplest treatment methods are needed because we cut our flowers and take them to market the same or the very next day. That means that our techniques for longer vase life can be simple, inexpensive, and very reliable. If you want to know more about the more esoteric methods of long term fresh flower storage and care, please refer to the bibliography section at the back of the book.

If I could stress just two points about cutting and handling flowers, they would be about water and cleanliness. For our purposes, and almost without exception, cut flowers must be given water to drink as soon as possible after cutting, and kept in clean water during their vase life. Most of the tricks about handling and harvesting of cut flowers are done to cause the flowers to take up and hold quantities of water in their tissues, because that is the way they will stay fresh-looking longer.

Many of the other precautions in handling cut flowers have to do with using clean clippers for harvesting and using clean containers for water and flower storage. The idea is to prevent the build up of bacteria which can lead to early wilting and flower loss.

Simple chemical preservatives are an important aspect to fresh flower preservation, and I would definitely advise their use during conditioning. Conditioning, by the way, is just a term used by florists to signify the post-harvest treatment of cut flowers in preparation for marketing. Preservatives—especially the ones with nutrients in them—can also help closed or partially open flowers to continue to mature and open up after cutting. But even if you choose never to use preservatives, you can keep a big lead on cut flower freshness by the quick use of water after cutting, the use of warm (100°-110°) water during the earliest stages of conditioning, and the careful control of bacteria in flower storage buckets and vases by extra cleaning and the use of a little bleach for added precaution.

Plant tissues are full of liquid during growth. Once cut from the mother plant the stems may wilt without the continuous taking up of water. I take a bucket of warm water and sometimes several buckets of different widths and depths to the garden with me to cut flowers. I keep the buckets in the shade and, as I cut the stems, add the flowers to a bucket that will keep those stems straight up and not bent over. I often mix the flowers in each bucket, cut almost every stem as long as possible, and all the time I'm cutting, I'm thinking about which of these flowers will go well together in bouquets. This becomes such a part of the ritual that, by the time I'm through cutting, I have a pretty good idea of how many bouquets I have flowers for, and an idea of what those bouquets are going to look like. But that only came about after a year of doing it and thinking about the flower arrangements as I was cutting. At first you may just end up with a feeling of jumbled buckets of flowers that you have to make some sense of.

I use either a sharp knife or small clippers for the cutting and wipe them off with bleach before using. I pick flowers in the morning or late afternoon as the flowers are in their best condition then, before or after the heat of the day. And I try to cut the stems on a slight angle in order to make it easier for them to drink the water in the bucket. Either at the time of picking or when I take the flowers to my laundry work room, I strip the stems of leaves so they will not rot in the water and cause bacteria to form in the buckets. Many florists also re-cut their flower stems under water after receiving flowers from the wholesaler. This keeps air bubbles from forming in the stems, but I have never done this. I also know several flower growers who sell bouquets without doing as much conditioning as I do and continue to do a fine business. The secret, of course, is the freshness of our flowers: direct to the buyer within a day or two of being cut in our gardens. That's so very much faster than almost any flowers available through ordinary commercial channels.

Knowing when to cut each flower can seem a bit intimidating but generally speaking you cut as soon as you know that most of the full flower stem will open after cutting. This is often when buds are just beginning to show their color. But for some plants it can mean cutting after every blossom on the stem has opened; for others it's when a half or even a quarter of the stem blossoms have opened. This information is also listed in the Cut Flower Catalog.

What about instructions for those plants that are not listed in the Catalog? For any new plant you wish to test, just try picking one at an early stage, putting it in warm water, with or without some preservative, and watching it at room temperature for a few days. I also use this method to try out greens and flowers I pick from the wild: put them in a vase with warm water and a little preservative (if you are using it) and watch them at room temperature to see how long they last. If they do O.K. for a few days with no other treatment, I know they'll do just fine in bouquets. It's also important to remember that many of the flowers you pick in the wild may need their stems split before putting them in the warm water and preservative. More about this in the next section.

If you try something new and it wilts in a day or so, you can either give up on it and move on to other things or try examining the plant more carefully to see if it has a hollow stem, or some milky sap that may be blocking the stem so it cannot take up water. Read through the whole section on harvest and conditioning and see if you can figure out where your new plant fits in. Some flowers simply will not keep for more than a day or two once they are cut from the plant and no amount of treatment or fussing will help them. Some may need later picking.

After I've picked the flowers I'm going to use for a bouquet delivery, I take them into my laundry room and proceed to finish stripping off any extra leaves from the stem bottoms, separate the flowers by type into small buckets, and place them in warm (100°-110°) water. This warm water forces open the stem tissues and helps the plants drink the water. I let them stand in the warm water for about an hour or so and then put them in the refrigerator until ready to do my arranging for market. It's very important that no fruit or vegetables be in the refrigerator because of the ethylene gas they produce and the harm to cut flowers from those gases. Ethylene causes a quick ripening or maturity in cut flowers that leads to early wilting.

I put the preservatives in the buckets I'm using to take the flowers to market. Floral preservatives come in several formulations and some of them are made for only one or two types of flower. But a basic one, such as Floralife™ can be used with almost all cut flowers and can be purchased at a wholesale florist supply house in any large city. Tell the clerks at the supply house what you're using it for and they will recommend the best one for you.

Until you are certain you're going to continue in the cut flower business, it's easy to substitute home-made preservative formula that will work quite well.

Here are a couple of recipes to try.

#1. Add 1/2 teaspoon chlorine bleach to a can of regular 7-Up™ in each bucket.

#2. Add 1 tablespoon of ordinary sugar, 2 tablespoons of lemon juice, and 2 teaspoons of bleach to a quart of water in each bucket.

The commercial formulas are probably better and are certainly easier to use. The wholesale price in my area right now for a ten pound bucket of Floralife is $20.65. Use one tablespoon to a quart of water, which makes the bucket good for 500 quarts, or 500 or more bouquets. Some bouquet sellers use small packets of Floralife that they attach to each bouquet for home use. These sell at about $20 wholesale for 250 little packets.

The flower conditioning you do at home determines the life of the bouquet in the buyer's home and also the repeat business you will get from that buyer. "These bouquets last so long at home." That's what you want people saying about your flowers. Spend time conditioning the flowers and it will pay off in sales.

✼

There are several special tricks to handling certain types of stems and flowers after cutting. Those are mentioned in the Catalog, but I'll give a few details on those methods now so that you'll know what is meant in the listings.

CONDITIONING WOODY STEMS

In the past it was recommended that these be pounded with a hammer at the stem ends to allow more water to be taken up. But that leads to bacterial growth and these days it is recommended that woody stemmed plants be cut into vertically at the stem ends with a clean sharp knife and then placed in warm water. Two cuts per stem are even better, but be careful doing this; I've got a bad scar or two from cutting my fingers along with the stems. Using a cutting board for this operation is a help to me. I also usually scrape off the outermost bark on woody stems along the bottom inch or so. Remember that if you later shorten the stems in your arrangements, you need to stop and re-cut the ends of these woody plants.

I have also noticed that woody stemmed plants are slower to drink water and I often use hotter water on them than I do on ordinary stems. Sometimes, if they start to wilt after a half hour or so, I'll change the water and add fresh, very warm water again to the bucket—just to force the stems to take up water.

HOLLOW STEMS

Delphiniums and hollyhocks are two that need this special care. Prick any hollow stem once near the blossom with a pin. Then turn the stem over, fill it with water and plug it with a piece of cotton or a bit of florist foam like *Oasis*. These flowers will last much longer if you take a moment or two to do this little trick. Everything you do is to get the flower to take up as much water as possible and hold it in the stem and blossom.

FLOWERS WITH SAP

Oriental poppies need a special treatment, and there are others plants like them that ooze a milky fluid which seals up the stem ends and prevents the flower from drinking water. Just after cutting poppies, I place the stem end over a flame for 20 or 30 seconds and sear the stem bottoms. I keep a candle in my workroom and light

Oriental poppy

that when I'm doing a batch of poppies. If you can't do this right after cutting, cut the stems again when you can sear them. And they must be re-burnt if you cut the stems when doing an arrangement. It's a bit of trouble, certainly, but poppies won't keep at all without this treatment and they are such outstanding flowers that they are worth the extra moments taken. They are almost never available through commercial florists and oriental poppies in a market bouquet will cause them to be snapped up by customers, as they are so handsome and unusual.

As I said in the beginning of this part, there are many other esoteric ways to treat fresh cut flowers to make them last a long time. But for a bouquet business or for almost any other small flower business like the ones we are talking about in this book, these steps for freshness are all you need. If you get into acreage growing you'll only do so with your markets clearly identified ahead of time, and at that time you may be asked by flower wholesalers or brokers to use more elaborate techniques in flower preservation. More likely they would be prepared to do such treatments and handling themselves.

FORCING FLOWERING BRANCHES

Blooming tree branches can make the most exciting additions to your bouquets, or they can be sold separately as very early, even winter bouquets, at a time when anything blooming is considered nearly priceless—just the attitude we flower sellers love to encourage.

The rule of thumb is that branches cut in January will take three weeks to flower, those cut in February will flower in two weeks, and those cut in March will flower in a week. That's in fairly normal weather.

For bouquets, I would stick to the February and March cuts for early bouquets so that you don't end up selling branches that won't bloom. Or else make the earlier branches part of a bouquet that doesn't require the branch to flower to make the arrangement effective. With daffodils or the other earlier bulbs, budded shrub or tree branches can add a lovely line and handsome color that doesn't really require that the branches burst into bloom to make the bouquet work.

If you only cut a few budding branches a year from your trees and shrubs, you probably don't have to worry too much about what you are taking. But if you become at all serious about harvesting these bare branches from shrubs and trees—especially from your fruit bearing trees—you should definitely have a good book on pruning and a good guide on shrubbery so that you don't end up doing any damage to your trees and shrubs. Pruning can be somewhat complicated, and knowing which branches will produce flowers and/or fruit becomes very important if you intend to harvest more than bare branches that year from your tree or shrub.

Always use very clean clippers or pruners when cutting the branches, and strip the outer bark from the bottom inch or so of the stem. Then split the stem

Flowering branch

bottoms at least once or twice so they can take up water easily.

Place the cut branches flat in warm, deep water right after they are cut—a bath tub works fine. Leave them there for an hour or two and then put the branches upright in fairly deep cold water for overnight, if possible. Bouquets of tree branches sell best for me when taken to market just before the buds begin to open. I have found that many customers don't think the branches will bloom unless they can actually see the color of the petals in the bud, or the first catkins are open, in the case of pussy willow. Make a habit of examining your budding branches almost daily if you intend to use them for sale; the changes are critical and occur quickly.

There are many shrubs and trees that can be forced to bloom early. You can try anything in your yard that looks interesting, and then see how well they do in your own home before you try selling them.

Here is a list of recommended varieties to harvest.

Acer Maple
Aesculus Horse Chestnut
Amelanchier canadensis Serviceberry

Azalea
Cercis canadensis Red Bud
Chaenomeles lagenaria Flowering Quince
Cornus florida Flowering Dogwood
Crataegus Hawthorn
Daphne
Forsythia
Hamamelis mollis Witch-hazel
Kalmia latifolia Mountain Laurel
Leucothoe
Magnolia
Malus Crab apple and apple
Philadelphus Mock-Orange
Prunus Flowering Fruit Trees
Rhododendron
Rhus canadensis Sumac
Salix Willow
Spirea
Syringa Lilac
Wisteria

PUTTING IT ALL
TOGETHER

The final steps in bouquet preparation have to do with arranging the flowers to take to market. Here again I must say that lots of people do this differently and most have real success, so I'll just describe my methods and let you take it from there.

The thought of doing a little "designing" with flowers may strike you as the most fun of this whole business, or else it may be a terrifying idea you'd like to avoid altogether. Those of you with the first reaction don't need a lot of help from me. So I'll direct most of my comments to the others who might be intimidated by having to put flowers together in an attractive way.

I'm one of the most non-visual people you would ever know. If I meet and talk to you for an hour, and then you walk away and someone else asks me what you were wearing or what you looked like, I simply couldn't answer. But I would have a lot to say about what I think you were feeling, or thinking or worrying about. I take in so much through my ears—so very little through my eyes. But whenever I've had to do a little designing in my life I have been able to do so by the use of a few tricks. I'll pass those along for whatever they're worth.

Get some books and magazines from the library on floral design and arrangements. Just keep looking at them, taking in the pictures over and over again until they become a part of your mental reference. Most will discuss the basic floral design terms like line and mass, which may or may not interest you, but just looking at the pictures of how bouquets are put together in homes will help you more than anything. You want your bouquets to look like they would be easy to take home, put in a vase and look very nice. After all, many of your customers won't know any more about designing and arranging than you do. So it is only important that your bouquets look *arrangeable*—not they you have every single part thought out and done for them.

Now take some time to play around with your cut flowers by placing some in a vase, moving them around, changing and re-changing the colors and types of flowers. Notice what happens when you add filler flowers, or greenery, a tall stem of cattail, or some white daisies. All of these things change the bouquet a little or a lot. To me, for instance, adding white daisies to a bouquet is like adding white collar and cuffs to a dressy dress. It suddenly becomes very sporty looking. It's totally changed. Or notice how adding stems of German statice to a bouquet of Siberian iris suddenly softens and changes it into something far less formal. Then try columbine with the iris and see how different that looks. Try something else—back and forth until you see yourself how you can make changes from something that looks O.K. to something that is very fine.

Always use one, three, or five special flowers in the bouquet (like dahlias, or peonies, for instance), because

Dahlia

using two or four is less interesting visually. Using even numbers seems to remove any sense of tension in the design. Try this yourself and see what I mean.

Make some bouquets for your home and see how people react to them, and how you react to them yourself after looking at them awhile. And here is a good place to mention what a boon the flower garden is for friendships and taking floral presents to friends. Once you begin selling flowers your friends will suddenly look on your floral offerings as something quite special. I buy vases at garage sales very cheaply and always have some on hand for taking bouquets to friends. They almost always bring them back, hoping, I think, that I'll refill them soon.

The best teacher of floral design is the garden, and the more time you spend observing flowers in the garden, the easier it will be to make up lovely bouquets. Start noticing individual flowers more closely; let your eye sweep across the flower bed noticing how one kind of blossom is offset or complemented by another. How one flower is dramatic and another frilly or informal.

When you see a flower arrangement anywhere, stop and really look at it. Attend some flower and garden shows in your area. Perhaps you've spent very little time at such things in the past, so now you need to make some room in your brain for this new way of looking. Slowly but surely you'll get more relaxed about it and, after your bouquets start selling, you'll realize there's really not that much to worry over.

Be certain to look carefully at each bouquet before taking it to market and make sure that there are no "uglies" in it. No brown leaves, dead flower buds, slug-eaten greens, and so forth. We get used to seeing (or rather not seeing) these things in our gardens; but they don't look very appealing in a floral bouquet for sale. Most shoppers want everything they buy to look as perfect as possible.

Once I'm ready to prepare the flowers for market, I set out all the buckets of flowers, start choosing and sorting, putting them into batches (in other buckets or even in vases) and deciding what to put together in a bouquet. At first this may seem to go very slowly, but in time you'll loosen up and be able to go much faster.

I use cellophane floral paper which I purchase from the wholesale florist house for about $5 for a 200 foot roll. It's 20" wide. I usually keep six colors on hand and use a mix of colors each time I take a group of bouquets to market. This is another of those personal choices—most people who sell bouquets don't bother with fancy paper. But I think it adds something special and also makes it very easy for someone to pick up one of your bouquets and take it along as a present for someone else. It also allows me to raise my prices because I'm offering something extra.

I roll off a little of the paper, fold one corner over to meet the opposite edge and cut it off in a 20" square. I then lay the paper on the top of my washing machine

and, with one of the corner points facing up, I fold the bottom quarter of the paper up and place the flowers and greens I want to use in the paper. I then wrap the bouquet with the paper and put a piece of *twist'em* around the whole thing. It's all very awkward the first few times you do it, but it does get easier and faster, and pretty soon you'll find you can arrange and wrap ten bouquets in something like twenty or thirty minutes.

I put preservative in clean buckets that I'm taking to market, add clean water and, if I'm not going to market immediately, put the buckets in the refrigerator over-night or until I am ready to take them to the store. I also mark and place a little colored circle sticker on each cellophane wrapper giving the price of each bouquet. I use a waterproof marker so it will not wash off before the customer buys the bunch. The usual price range is four to ten dollars depending entirely on what's in the bouquet. The more unusual and "expensive" the main flowers are, the higher the price. You'll probably make your bouquet prices too low at first, but after you see them start to sell you'll realize what a bargain you are giving and raise them up a dollar or two. I think almost any bouquet is worth five dollars or more these days. The buckets can hold four to six bouquets and I usually take two buckets in at a time.

You can use any clean, fairly shallow bucket to take the bouquets to market, but one thing that may happen is that the buckets get emptied and someone in the market picks them up for some other use. So it's probably smart to mark or paint the buckets ("Locally Grown Flowers", perhaps) in order to try to hang on to them.

Put plenty of water in your buckets when you take them to the store. And check back in a day or two to be sure they still have water in them. Some flowers can drink up so much water so fast that you'll be surprised to see how quickly the water level in the buckets goes down. I usually get water in the store for adding to the buckets.

Look also to see if the bouquets should be consolidated in one bucket. When you get down to only two or three bouquets, you'll want to bring some fresh ones in and remove any that don't look just right. Don't count on the store clerks to do any of this. They have too much else to look after.

If you do have any returns you have to show that on the invoice and have it signed just as you would a delivery. Make a special line on the invoice page for returns so you can have that signed and then adjust the price at the end of the pay period.

Pay special attention to any bouquets that don't get purchased. Ask yourself why they weren't bought. Were they too skimpy or had the flowers wilted a little? You can learn something from any returns you have so as not to make the same mistakes again. Incidentally, it may take a week or more for your flowers to begin selling very well—it sometimes takes that long for customers to get used to something new and be willing to try it. You will notice after a while that the same people come back to buy your flowers over and over again. They will see you making deliveries and speak to you, get your phone number from the produce manager and call you for flowers for a special occasion, and somehow let you know that they think you are doing a good job. I'm always delighted when they do. People who have the flower habit really have it.

One other important way to sell flowers in the market is by the stem. Many people would like to do their own flower arranging, and want only to be supplied with stems of flowers, period.

Flowers by the stem are what you sell when you have quite a big bunch of one kind of flower and can take them to market in a special bucket, or even a gallon jar with a single stem price on them. Delphiniums, for instance, at $1.00 to $1.50 each; lilies at $1.50 a stem; baby's breath at $1.00 per stem (or more, depending on the fullness); Sweet Williams at 35¢ each, gladiolus at $1.25 per stem, etc. All of these prices are just suggestions and should be determined by you based on the price and availability in your area. These single stems sell easily, take very little time to prepare and are quite profitable.

꽃

If you want to try some other display for your flowers, you might check out the florist supply house near you, as we did, and see if there is something that your store would agree to use. Often the supply house will have pictures they can give you of display items and you can show these to the store you are talking to. Just walking through the supply house can give you many ideas to try.

In fact, I recommend that you make a trip to your wholesale florist while you are considering the flower business and just where you might fit in. They are usually large warehouses in downtown areas that open up very, very early in the morning to deal with fresh cut flower and plant deliveries. They deal with florists in a large region and supply them with much more than flowers. Their warehouse will be chock full of vases and pots of every description and size, Christmas decorations if you visit in the fall, Easter frillery if you go there in the spring. Candles, balloons by the zillion, wreath making supplies, potpourri makings, stuffed birds and coffee mugs—absolutely anything at all they think a florist shop might want to use or try to sell.

They also sell a large selection of both dried flowers and silk flowers. Often, in a fairly large city, there will be several floral supply shops, each one specializing in different items, each one with their own special customers, growers, and suppliers.

A wholesale florist differs from a flower broker in that the wholesaler has this warehouse full of goods where the flower shop owner (and the public) can come wandering in and see what is available, whereas the broker usually operates more of a purchasing or shipping facility only and seldom deals with any small florists. Both wholesalers and brokers are open to buying from new and small flower growers IF the growers can offer them something quite special. And always, they want very good quality. You will be meeting some of these people in the next part of the book.

Now perhaps you will want to try a bouquet business of your own as it is one of the easiest small businesses you can run from home, and one of the most pleasant. I think I've given you enough information on selling bouquets to get you started if that is the direction you want to go. But, as I've been saying, there are many different approaches to selling flowers.

OTHER WAYS TO SELL YOUR FLOWERS

Besides the market business, I have also sold flowers for special occasions—primarily weddings and parties—and I definitely recommend that you try this too, if you can grow enough flowers. In fact, some growers choose only to do these special occasion flowers and don't bother with the bouquet business. Or they sell at the local Saturday market and also arrange and sell flowers for special occasions.

A tiny ad in the classifieds can bring many calls:

FRESH CUT GARDEN FLOWERS
FOR SPECIAL OCCASIONS
Your Telephone Number

You can use your own vases or have your customers bring theirs. I usually charge more for party arrangements in special vases because of the extra time and thought and flowers that can go into such an effort, perhaps seven fifty to fifteen dollars each. If you have a knack for arranging and can supply many flowers, your prices can go much, much higher for these special occasion bouquets.

Wedding bouquets are often much more elaborate and are also very good business for flower growers. Make sure you are really prepared for this as wedding flowers can be a rather involved time—and flower—consuming specialty. You will meet wedding flower growers in our interviews. They offer much information.

My suggestion to anyone interested in the wedding market is to supply wedding flowers for a friend or relative and see just what is involved. Who provides the containers? How many flower items and bouquets are needed? How much time do you need to prepare the presentation? How much help is required? Can you handle the stress of such an event? There is definitely a lot of wedding business out there for garden flower growers—but it is a much more intense, almost show-off kind of business and will not suit everyone. For those who enjoy it, this can offer some of the very best money available in garden flowers.

If you decide to give it a try, I would first of all contact the people at any resorts, hotels, or fancy restaurants near you where wedding ceremonies and receptions are held and find out if you can become one of the people they recommend for wedding flowers. Inquire at your local churches to see if they make recommendations to people who are having weddings there. Visit the shops that cater to brides and get acquainted. Put a little classified ad in your local paper.

Perhaps your garden itself is a real showplace from your long term gardening efforts. You can consider renting it out for weddings or other special events.

There are many other little special niches for flowers grown for cutting and selling. In my culinary herb business, I grew and sold edible cut flower blossoms to the restaurant trade in my area. I assumed at the time (three or four years ago) that it was a food fad that would quickly pass. Actually, I notice nowadays that edible blossoms as garnish, or edible flowers in "European" or "Wild Seasonal Salads" are still very, very popular in certain specialty restaurants and that the 'fad' is lasting quite a bit longer than I thought it would.[2]

Because of my membership in the Association of Specialty Cut Flower Growers,[3] I recently received a letter from a company in New York called "Flowers of the Week", who have a weekly marketing sevice in New York, Connecticut and New Jersey and who "avidly seek new and different material for our clients." I didn't call them, but if I had a field of cut flowers, I certainly would.

Let us move out a little further now and see where else you might sell your cut flowers. One very obvious place where home grown flowers will be welcome is at your local florist shop. Many florists, particularly those in rural areas who have to get their flower supply from some distance, will welcome the chance to buy garden fresh flowers of certain kinds. And, unless you live in a very conservative area, your florist is aware of the demand for old-fashioned garden flowers vs. the more traditional flowers they are accustomed to working with—namely, carnations, roses, and mums.

You should, first of all, get acquainted with your local florists and let them know what you are growing. They can let you know what days of the week or times of the month they might be interested in looking at what you have. They may even want to visit your garden and talk flowers with you. Some shop owners are very crazy about flowers. Others, believe it or not, really aren't.

A florist would want to buy either by the bunch or a bucketful, but they will want very long stems and fairly high quality flowers. In florist arrangements, every single flower counts for something special and they cannot afford to purchase other than first quality blossoms. You offer local florists a couple of big advantages: your flowers are much, much fresher than anything they can get from their wholesaler, and you can deliver to them without a delivery charge.

As far as your pricing to them is concerned, they can help you with that as they buy flowers every day. But you should learn something about pricing yourself by visiting your area wholesale florists and learning what wholesale prices are being paid for flowers. The prices vary almost daily depending on what's available, of course, but you can get an idea of the range from a wholesaler and by visiting several florists in your area. Getting acquainted with your local florists can also help you determine what it is they are looking for and wishing that a local grower could provide for them. The price you get should be one that makes selling to the florist shop seem worthwhile. Otherwise, if the price seems too low to you, you would be better off choosing another way to market your flowers. By the time you get to the end of this book, you should know of many ways you can market your flowers.

This brings up another business detail that needs to be covered if you choose any of these other methods for flower selling. It is important that you understand the difference between wholesale and retail selling and, depending on where you live, the difference that can make in the prices you charge, the taxes you may have to pay, or the business licenses you need.

If you sell your flowers to a family putting on a wedding, they are the end customer and therefore you have made a retail sale. If, on the other hand, you sell those same wedding flowers to a caterer who is putting on a wedding and offering the flowers as one of his or her services, you have made a wholesale sale—to the caterer, who then sells to the end customer, the wedding family. In any state that has a sales tax, this distinction is of primary importance.

In the first instance where you sell to the end, or final customer, the actual consumer of the flowers, you would be responsible to the state to collect the sales tax from the customer. In the second instance, the caterer would be responsible for that tax collection. And the price of the goods doesn't matter. The caterer, for instance, could charge the wedding customer much more, or exactly what you have charged the caterer for the flowers. They could even charge them less. But the one who sells to the end or final customer, to the customer who will actually be using the goods and not reselling them, is the one responsible for collecting the sales taxes and sending them in to the state.

It is this agreement to collect taxes for the state that you must keep if you live in a state with a sales tax and you do any retail selling. The agreement is usually made in the form of a business license from the state to you. The license is issued by the state, is often quite inexpensive, and legally binds you to collect a certain percentage of each sale from each retail customer you have and send that money to the state every few months, or at least once a year.

One positive note in all of this tax collecting talk is that this same license to sell at retail also gives you the right to buy at wholesale—and that can have many advantages, of course. The resale license number from the state allowing you to sell flowers to a retail customer means that that same number allows you to buy plants, tools, even furniture or anything else at wholesale prices IF you can meet the quantity purchase requirements of the companies you want to buy from.

If you should get one of these wholesale licenses (which allow you to sell retail) you will immediately notice a little marginal world that exists at many manufacturing and supply businesses around the country. They advertise themselves as a wholesale business and yet they will sell to retail customers, too. And the price customers pay depends strictly on quantities involved. If you are a retail customer at one of these stores and you don't have a resale number, you will be charged sales tax.

Although it's true that you may be asked for this number at a wholesale florist house if you want to buy supplies, it's just as likely you can probably buy supplies there without that number. You just may pay more for your purchases, and you will definitely have to pay retail sales taxes if your state has them. I have a wholesale number, and find it very helpful in many ways.

✤

Now that I've told you what I know about flower selling from my garden, let's start our visits to other growers and see what they are up to. Many are much more experienced than I.

---

[2] For a full list of edible flowers see *Profits From Your Backyard Herb Garden*. Ordering information can be found in the back of this book.

[3] See "Associations," page 184.

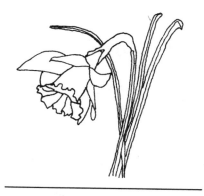

ISLAND FLOWER
GROWERS

I live on one of the San Juan Islands in Puget Sound, off
the coast of Washington State. There is a small but fairly
sophisticated population; plus a much larger population
in the summertime when tourists come here from all over
the country (and the world). It's a boating community, a
very outdoor oriented community, and there are several
people on this island and the other islands nearby who
are growing and selling flowers. Before I introduce you to
flower growers in other states and areas, I'd like you to
meet the other flower growers in my own county. They
all have interesting stories to tell, and they sell their
flowers in ways you may be able to imitate.

When I stopped selling flowers at the local supermarket to do other things, one of my friends, Mary
Karen Ryan, started taking her flowers to market. She
has also been selling flowers on the island for a few years
in other, interesting ways.

The island has several Bed & Breakfast Inns which
are kept very busy during the season. The Inn owners
appreciate Mary Karen's delivery of a bucket of flowers
once or twice a week, so that they can keep fresh flowers

in their guest rooms. The B&B owners do all the arranging, so Mary Karen finds this an easy, pleasant way to sell flowers. She charges six to ten dollars a bucket depending on what flowers she takes.

She has also been delivering bouquets to offices and stores in the town of Friday Harbor. She takes them in cut-off milk cartons, and the shopkeepers and office workers supply their own vases. This office floral service has not been as satisfactory to her as the B&B service, mainly because of the time spent arranging the flowers and because of all the time spent delivering—finding a place to park and getting in and out of her car. The car, incidentally, is usually full of very young children—Mary Karen's two little boys and their friends. But she realizes it could become a much more profitable service if she were to raise her prices and work out the delivery details more carefully. She knows that the office bouquet service idea has real potential because when she started calling on people to see if they were interested in such a service, no one ever turned her down.

Her garden, by the way, is a plot in her backyard, 50'x100', which she keeps intensively planted in both perennials and annuals. She finds flower growing and selling is the one thing she can do well that allows her to stay home with her children and still earn some money. She also happens to have a passion for growing flowers.

Her latest project involved going to the County Planning Department last spring with a proposal for a little unmanned flower stand she wants to have built and installed in front of her husband's veterinary clinic on one of the main arterial roads coming into Friday Harbor. Final approval came through recently and now she's talking to builders and making plans for installing it in a few months. She's been learning to make wreaths and wonders about the possibility of selling them in the stand during the fall and winter. Her children sell pumpkins in October and next year they will be able to sell them at the flower stand.

Mary Karen thinks she will be charging four dollars a bouquet at the stand the first year, and that she will need to run a classified ad in the local paper announcing the stand, and perhaps have to keep the ad going the first season or two until everyone realizes it's there.

☙

Frank and Vicki Giannangelo opened San Juan Island's first real herb farm a few years ago, and now visitors to Giannangelo Farms: Organic Vegetables and Culinary Herbs, can also purchase bouquets of flowers there as Frank and Vicki have planted flowers in patterns throughout the herb gardens. Tulips and daffodils, dahlias, glads, snaps and salpiglossis, plus many everlasting flowers that Vicki dries and sells along with the herbs, vinegars, and other herbal products she makes. She will pick flowers to order for her customers.

The farm itself has been cut out from the center of very deep woods; one has only to look around and realize what a truly difficult job they must have had in opening up this sunny, delightful garden which is still surrounded by thick woods.

A wedding gazebo is also featured in the garden design and the first wedding was held there this summer—a trial run, says Vicki, of what they realize can become a popular wedding location on the island.

When we talked she was grateful that they had just apparently solved the big problem for northwest growers—a way to eliminate slugs from the garden. Last spring they laid a twelve inch strip of cedar sawdust

Lily

around the garden perimeters and then ran a thin line of rock salt down the center of the strip. The slugs would not cross over the salt. It is a tremendous success, said Vicki, and now they are in the process of putting a little cover over the barrier so that the northwest rains won't destroy the effectiveness of it.

Frank and Vicki also sell flowers at our island Saturday market; and Vicki, in typical small town style, recently made floral headbands for a local little theater production of "How Green Was My Valley."

Not too far from the Herb Farm, Lesa Waldron oversees a home filled with three children, a large greenhouse full of potted plants, and a field full of cut flowers. It's all part of Amity Gardens, Lesa's work for the past eight years on the family's seven acres.

The primary horticulture business is one of selling potted plants both to customers who come to the gardens and to stores and nurseries on the mainland. Lesa sells tens of thousands of potted plants each season and, over the years, has planted out leftover perennials which have formed the backbone of her large cutting garden. She sells what she calls "country bouquets" at her gardens—very large bunches of assorted garden flowers for five dollars per bunch. She also delivers buckets of flowers to several restaurants in the area and prices those at twenty dollars for a five gallon bucket of cut blossoms. In the summer months, she also sells her bouquets at one of the local markets.

Lesa used to do weddings but gave them up a year or so ago, "because they are just too stressful—people are too uptight at weddings." She has also dropped an interest she had in making wreaths of dried flowers, "because too many people got into them."

Her concentration on potted plants is paying off with increased business every year, and she now supplies the local landscapers with much of what they need for their work here on the island. But she has no intention of giving up flower growing. It's a perfect fit with the potted plant business, and it seems certain that one of these days she'll have the whole seven acres planted in flowers.

❧

One of the larger flower growers in my area who sells many different ways, including to florists, is Gary Franco of Lopez Island. Gary started out seven years ago as a strawberry grower and, over the years, has added cut flowers to his crops. Like most of the other growers I have talked to, Gary sees the flower market as one that is increasing rapidly. Now, year by year, he gives more of his acreage to it.

He tries to sell all he can at retail because he earns more that way. He sells flowers at the famous public market in Seattle, called Pike Place Market, and also at farmer's markets in Redmond and in Fremont, both in the Seattle area.

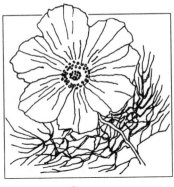

Cosmos

His flower crops include Dutch iris, which can be temperature controlled and retarded in storage, so that he can have iris blooming from spring all the way through the season until hard frost. He also grows lots of Asiatic lilies, gladiolus, cosmos, snaps and statice—all field grown.

Over the years, he has also developed about thirty florist accounts that he keeps in touch with and sells to at different times of the year. Gary grows daffodils and tulips for the very early market and says he can usually get a good price from florists because he can deliver flowers that are so much fresher than they can buy elsewhere. He and his wife, Alberta, do much of the work, but have from three to fifteen helpers at different times of the year.

How does he determine the price for his flowers, I wondered. "If I don't know the price", he says, "I just call a Seattle flower wholesaler and ask. They will tell me the price on the phone. After a while, you just know." And he always asks a little more than the wholesale price because of that extra freshness he can offer along with no extra charge for delivering to the shops.

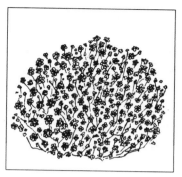

Gypsophilia (Baby's Breath)

The Francos still grow berries of different kinds both for a U-Pick and for stores. Additionally they have developed a line of delicious jams and preserves that they are selling at the farmer's markets and to retail stores in the Northwest. Gary also sets up a booth at the county fair selling both cut flowers and heavenly ice cream and berry sundaes. Sometimes he will just park his truckload of berries and flowers along one of our town streets and sell to islanders as they pass by on their way to and from town.

❧

Next to Gary's farm on Lopez is Arbordoun Farm, where Susan Bill has been growing flowers for years and setting a hard work example for all of us. Her deep interest in medicinal herbs led her a few years ago to concoct a wonderful herbal hand cream for gardeners called Calendula Cream that she now sells all across the nation. She grows an acre or so of flowers that she sells both fresh at the market on her island and as dried flowers to a distributor in Seattle. At the local market, she displays her bouquets in a small nine cone flower stand where they sell for five dollars a bunch, with 30% going to the market.

Susan also does a fairly busy wedding business supplying flowers for ten or fifteen weddings per summer on Lopez. She charges, on average, about three hundred and fifty dollars per wedding which would include a bridal bouquet, corsages for the wedding party members, boutonierres for the men, and bouquets for the bridesmaids, plus two to four arrangements for the ceremony itself. She provides baskets and vases for the parties.

Susan is like the other island flower growers in that she keeps several interests going at once. Besides the herbal products, growing flowers for both the fresh and dried markets and supplying flowers for island weddings, she also tends about three hundred and fifty apple trees which are espaliered along her driveway coming into the farm. For years, she grew and sold organically grown garlic for the California market. But cut flowers have always been one of her primary crops.

✻

The key point I learned in writing this book on cut flowers is that it is all about niche finding: seeking out one or more little corners of the enormous world-wide flower market where you can fit in and sell your cut flowers. There are more niches than I ever imagined, and once you begin looking for them you may be surprised to find some unusual ones in your own back yard.

That's the feeling I had recently when I saw a two-line classified ad in my local paper wanting to purchase flower blossoms. I responded, of course, and found Bill Carli, owner and operator of Island Flower Pictures. He runs an unusual manufacturing company that creates and markets calligraphy quotations surrounded by pressed, dried flower arrangements. The quote and the flowers are carefully set into a 4"x6" or 8"x10" glass frame and shipped to department stores and gift shops all over the country.

Mr. Carli's business is growing. He now ships fifteen to twenty thousand of these framed pictures a year and sometimes he simply runs out of blossoms. He ran the local ad because he was having a hard time finding enough blossoms to do his orders. Each picture can take up to twenty or more small dried flowers.

Bill grows fifteen flower varieties himself and has people both growing and collecting flowers in the wild for him. His growers are primarily in Oregon, but he would like to have some local ones, too. He teaches his growers the tricks of learning to harvest correctly, and then pressing and drying the blossoms so that they are just right for the pictures.

Bill is quick to point out that no one can really get rich growing blossoms for him, but he claims he keeps several people in Oregon in "Bingo money" and wishes he could find more growers and pickers.

My own neighborhood growers taught me what a varied world this flower sales business is, so I set off to interview people in other regions to see just how far the idea can be taken. What's really out there for small growers, I wondered, and how hard is it to get a foothold in the larger market? I think you will be intrigued as I was with the answers to that question.

PART II

TALKING FLOWERS

A MONEY
HEDGE

Sometimes you can fit a small horticultural operation into your landscape with such finesse that no one would ever guess you were snipping money from your hedgerows.

Just such a clever deceit awaits the visitor at the home of Al and Genevieve Schultz in the rock-strewn foothills behind Escondido in northeast San Diego county. A long, uphill asphalt drive runs along the Schultz avocado grove (which is leased to another avocado grower) and leads up to the house. Between the grove and the drive is a three foot high hedge of colorful *Leptospermum* also known as Australian Tea Tree, a prized florist filler of white and rosy sprays of long lasting flowers. It's a nice hedge and fits into the landscape perfectly.

Another hedge begins at the top of the driveway, curves around the front of a patch of green grass, and neatly separates the house from the avocado grove. This one is waxflower (*Chamaelaucium uncinatum*), also a favored plant of florists everywhere.

Al and Genevieve Schultz are a vigorous healthy looking retired couple living a bit of a dream retirement that many people would envy. Suntanned from outside living, both are obvious workaholics who have created a little oasis in the sunny back country above Escondido.

Al Schultz served in the Philippines during World War II and noticed that everyone in the armed forces made a big fuss over avocados. He'd grown up in Southern California, where avocados were pretty ordinary fare, but he thought maybe someday he would retire there and become an avocado grower. That's just what he did do, but not until he'd spent many years working in Los Angeles in the television industry. His last job was as transportation co-ordinator for the long running TV series *Route 66*.

When the Schultzes finally settled into retirement several years ago in Valley Center, they put in the flower hedges because they were beautiful and because Al knew there just might be a chance to sell them if they grew well. They put in 160 *Leptospermum* plants and 75 waxflower plants. Two years later they began harvesting flowers and have earned money on them ever since. They were able to make such good choices on plants to raise because those particular plants were being raised in the neighborhood by another small commercial flower grower.

Al had had no farming experience but Genevieve was raised on a wheat farm in North Dakota and had a great sense of what growing and seasons were all about. The avocados, of course, have been their primary crop but the flowers have added extra money to their income year after year. From the beginning they have used the profits to buy savings bonds for their grandchildren, thereby avoiding any taxes on the money and giving their grandchildren (who now come and help with the harvesting) a fine sense of how to grow flowers for profit.

"We are probably the smallest commercial flower operation in the whole country," says Schultz, "but our grandkids think we're the greatest."

Harvesting of the flower stems begins in December—with much of the country deep in the heart of winter—and flower blossoms of almost any kind are welcome by everyone. Al and the other family members go out early in the morning or late in the evening in cool weather and actually prune their hedge to get the long stems of flowers at just the right stage. Their buyer, a local flower broker, has taught them just when to pick. They wrap the rather thick stems with a rubber band in bundles 1 1/2 inches in diameter and place the bundles in buckets of water immediately, ten bundles to the bucket. They don't refrigerate the flowers overnight if they pick in the evening but always take them immediately to the buyer early in the morning. They don't put anything in the buckets for conditioning. "The buyer does all that," says Al.

Waxflower and *leptospermum* are not very common garden flowers, having only become popular in the landscapes of hot and low rainfall areas in the last few years. But they have the qualities florists seek: long stems that are long lasting, plus very nice colors. These same qualities have also made them very popular floral crops, so they are now grown by large growers all around the sunny parts of the world.

When I first set out to investigate other small flower growers, I thought they would all be growing only unusual plants. Getting into varieties that "the big guys" are into would be the last thing a small grower would want to try. Or so I thought. Yet over and over I found small growers who do just that: choose to grow flowers that are grown in mass quantities, both domestically and abroad. And some of these little guys are quite successful. I also soon found out that the growers who succeed in these efforts are supreme niche finders. Most often that means making a good-fit connection with someone who needs and appreciates just what that small grower is doing.

The key to the success in the Schultz operation was finding a buyer who appreciated both the quality and dependability this small operation could offer. Making this good connection took some time—but the relationship has lasted for years. And the example is one that cannot be overemphasized: in the beginning, give a lot of attention to the selling of the flowers you want to grow.

Spend some time learning something about the marketing before you put too much effort into increasing your growing capacity. And that means, importantly, getting out and talking to possible buyers of your flowers. First of all, check the yellow pages of your area phone books and find the wholesale florist businesses—both brokers and wholesalers. Give them a visit or two to look over their operations (they are usually open early in the morning). You can learn a lot by just paying a visit. Talk to flower shop owners and operators and produce/flower buyers at supermarkets. Anyplace you see flowers being sold, you should be talking, talking, talking to the people involved.

In the little Schultz flower business, the culture of both of the hedge plants they grow is similar and relatively easy. Both plants originated in Australia, both can stand lots of heat and need relatively little water. Al installed a drip system when he put in the hedges but still finds water a big part of his thinking about growing anything in Southern California. Water rationing was about to begin there at the time of my visit and I found his driveway full of buckets of rain water he'd collected from some recent rare rainfalls. His grove and the flower hedges are on hillsides so he takes very special care not to waste any water in runoff.

At the time of my visit they were uncertain about just how limited their water supply would be. There was talk of a 50% cut for everyone in their situation, but it turned out a few days later to only be a 20% cut in water usage that was needed immediately. Now California seems to be in the process of taking away large amounts of irrigation water from some of their big farmers, which will free up water for continued development and smaller users. But any way you look at it, the water situation is very serious there and will require a long list of changes for many, many people.

And California is not the only state with water problems in the offing. The supply of good water at a reasonable price is of utmost importance for anyone considering a small cut flower operation. Even in the rainy state of Washington, our town reservoir has gone nearly dry twice in the last ten years. Drip systems, soaker hoses made from recycled tires, automated watering to cut down on waste—we're all looking into new ways to save what once seemed to be an unlimited resource. The cost, quality, and availability of water are now near the very top of the list of things to consider in thinking about a cut flower operation.

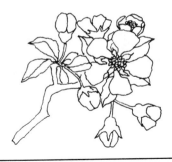

HARVESTING FLOWERS
FROM FRUIT TREES

"I had just one almond tree, and started complaining to my friend, Don, the flower broker, that I was going to rip the darn thing out because the birds beat me to the almonds every year. 'Don't be stupid' said Don, 'almonds bloom early. You can make some money with that tree.' I laughed at him, but he proved my stupidity by selling a hundred and fifty dollars worth of blossom stems off my tree the very next January. Needless to say, I became a convert."

Graham Baldree grew up on a tobacco farm in North Carolina, but spent most of his life working in electronics and managing rental property. He got back into horticultural efforts after an early retirement and a move to Escondido, California, where he started putting in some avocado and macadamia trees on his property. His friendship with a San Marcos flower broker got Graham going on his latest endeavor: growing deciduous flowering fruit trees for the fresh flower market.

In the middle of January and February, when most of the country is buried under grey moods and cold snow, Baldree can go to his fruit stem orchard and pick long stems of bud-swollen fruit branches for shipment all across the land. They burst into life and color in florist shops and homes everywhere and people happily pay good money for such a mid-winter pleasure.

At least that's the way it works when all goes well, weather-wise, on Baldree's one and a half acre fruit tree plot. He's got to have enough cold weather to help deciduous fruit trees flourish, and not so much cold that the buds don't swell in the middle of winter. He once had avocados planted on the north facing slope, but it was too cold for them. Two years ago he took them out to try the fruit trees in that spot.

"I'm still just learning," he says. "Every variety here is different, every tree has to be looked at and harvested at just the right time." He has three hundred trees of many different types so that kind of careful watching is not all that easy to do. The Bonita flowering apricot blooms after the Thunder Cloud flowering plum and the Akebono or Kwanzan flowering cherries. But each variety also seems to have late and early bloomers, so each stem of each tree has to be looked at very carefully to decide when to cut. Cut too early and the stems will never bloom—cut a day or two late and the stems will open up during shipping and the florists don't want them. Florists want to buy stems just before they open so that their customers will get the full benefit of long flowering.

What Baldree is trying for is to get each tree to produce 30 or 40 three- to four-foot-long stems every year. He has spent the first couple of years learning how to recognize the perfect time to cut each variety and then how to prune and cut back the trees for the best production the following year. If he misses a long stem (and it begins to bloom on the tree) he will cut that one hard back for the following year. The shorter stems he usually leaves alone, and finds that they will lengthen very well the next year.

He fertilizes the trees with a commercial 15-15-15 mix in April, July and October, but gives no feed or water in November or December. That's in order to stress the trees so they will begin putting out flower stems as early as possible. Last year's extra cold winter weather has delayed much of the bloom so that he missed the very early and very best market with much of his crop. "Anything you can take to market before Valentine's Day," he says, "is worth twice as much as it would be the week after. And we didn't get enough early budding this year. We can still sell them, of course, but the price goes down."

The price, he says, varies all over the place from two dollars a bunch to twenty dollars a bunch, depending on the length of the stems and the time of the year. Actually, the broker takes care of all the marketing of the stems and Baldree only worries about the trees—and the weather.

He cuts the stems with hand clippers early in the morning and wraps them in bundles of ten and takes the bundles almost immediately to the broker's warehouse a few miles away. Graham doesn't put the stems in water and knows that sometimes they are shipped right away by air without going into water at all. "I don't worry about any of that sales stuff," he says. "I'm just trying to learn what these trees do."

Graham Baldree is a gentle voiced, fast talking, hard working go-getter who is into an intense mental relationship with three hundred fruit trees growing on his land. He is concentrating with all he's got to try to get this endeavor to pay off in the way he now knows it can.

He feels he's got the yearly care worked out, plus the necessary weeding and an automated water system that puts a slow misty ten gallons per hour for eight hours on the trees. He has to do that every four or five days in summer. All of the trees are growing beautifully. What Baldree is concentrating on now is the harvesting and the realization that every tree must be visited every day during those winter and early spring months in order to look directly at every single stem and make a decision: is it ready or not? If I cut it today, will it open up at the right time? If I leave it for a day or two, will it be too late? Apricots, cherries, apples, pears, almonds, crabapples, peaches, nectarines—and more than one variety of each kind. Baldree is learning those trees the way he has to learn them: day by day, one by one, stem by stem. Yet he talks already of adding three hundred more trees as soon as he gets these all figured out.

ZUCCHINI TO
ZINNIAS

Sauvie Island (pronounced saw-vee) is a pastoral won-
derland—just the place to go for a beautiful summer bike
ride. It's also the perfect place to give a big family picnic,
go for a scenic drive, pick some strawberries, or buy some
wonderfully fresh vegetables. And pick a gorgeous bouquet! Flowers just the way you want them.

The island is the largest one in the Columbia River,
where the Willamette and Columbia Rivers run together
and where Oregon gives way to the Columbia with
Washington State on the other side. Sauvie Island was
an early outpost for the Hudson's Bay Company, has
long been a summer recreation retreat for swimming and
fishing for those in the Portland area, and a game man-
agement area for winter waterfowl.

For Dennis and Nancy Grandee and their family,
Sauvie Island is 145 acres and ten years of hard work
growing vegetables on their family farm. A big metal
shop building faces the dike road and is used to store and
ship the vegetable crops and also as a place to sell to retail
customers.

A few years ago Nancy turned the area in front of the

shop into a small field of flowers as a memorial to her parents, both deceased, whose graves Nancy seldom had time to visit. When she could find the time to go to the cemetery, she never had flowers to take along. So she planted the little flower field (mostly zinnias) to honor her parents and add another crop her vegetable customers might be interested in. Why not give it a try, she wondered. Why not, indeed.

Nowadays, on a summer day, a hundred and fifty people will make the trip to Sauvie Island and Nancy Grandee's flower field. And you would too, if you lived near there. She charges only ten cents for a mammoth zinnia three or four feet tall, only ten cents for cosmos, snapdragons, marigolds—anything she considers *ordinary*. And only 20, 30, or 40 cents for what she considers *special* flowers: gladiolus, lilies, Dutch iris, liatris.

Her system is a simple one with most of her efforts going into the growing part and very little worry given to the customer part. Most people who find her just keep coming back, and soon bring their own containers and their own clippers, although Nancy keeps some little buckets and clippers handy for the new customers. She simply turns people loose into the bright, colorful fields of flowers that have drawn them off the dike road for several years now.

"No, they really don't do a lot of damage," she claims, "although we are going to make our beds a little narrower this year, as I do sometimes find paths through the beds where they shouldn't be."

The customers bring the flowers in to the check-out counter, where they are counted out by the stem. And then off goes another happy customer with a week's supply of flowers for a very few dollars that Nancy Grandee is delighted to get in return. She feels the flower growing more than pays for the little space it uses and some of the flower buyers usually take home a few fresh vegetables, too.

"When I first started the flowers," she says, "the vegetable buyers would maybe sometimes pick up a few flowers to take home. That has really turned around now with the flower lovers holding their own."

Needless to say, some florists in the Portland area have now heard of Nancy and make regular trips to her field as they can purchase the freshest of flowers for less than they would pay wholesale in the flower markets. She sells to the florists at the same price as she does to anyone else.

Often whole families will come out to pick for a wedding party or other special event. It's the kind of a place you know will soon be written up in magazines: "A U-Pick Flower Field in a Great -Get-Away Setting."

They remain open seven days a week from May to November, help stage the Sauvie Island Market Strawberry Festival in June, offer pony rides and hay rides for Halloween, and try to keep island visitors coming for as many months as possible.

What's especially fun in talking to Nancy is her intense concentration on learning about flowers herself. She doesn't pretend to be an expert in something she fell into quite accidentally. She buys seeds from the Harris Co. (fine producers of vegetable seeds, too.) And she has a woman friend who sells flower starts and gives Nancy some good tips and guidance on what to try next in her fields. She's still learning the differences between annual, biennial, and perennial plants and how they act in the field. I got the feeling she was listening to me for any knowledge I might have on flowers, just as hard as I was listening to her tell of her own growing experiences.

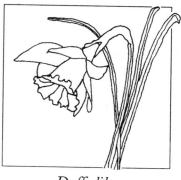

Daffodil

Every time she meets anyone who grows flowers she asks for their recommendations on what to grow.

Adjoining the flower fields are rows and rows of well tended boysenberry plants, blueberries, marion berries, strawberries, and rows of zucchinis leading to acres of every kind of vegetable imaginable. The zucchini, Nancy tells me, will be relocated at the end of the year to make room for a quarter acre of daffodils—another first effort on their part. It's obvious the flowers are gaining ground on the Grandee fields.

For this summer the flower season will consist of carnations (from starts), snapdragons, suworowii statice, German statice, Esther Reed daisies, delphiniums, yarrow, liatris, sunflowers, eucalyptus, gladiolus, marigolds, Chinese asters, cosmos, lilies, and the real crowd pleasers: tall, tall zinnias.

Like every other small grower I interviewed in the northwest, the Grandees are still suffering from losses of the terrible winter of '90-'91. That's when the north Pacific coast was hit with truly fierce storms (after weeks of rain) that simply wiped out acres and acres of the plants that usually grow in this mild climate.

The Grandee flower operation is still new enough to make Nancy worry about that kind of weather and everything else. But she's smart enough to see that flowers are a fine crop for a U-Pick and she works hard enough at it to tell me she'll make a real success of it.

I also realized that a U-Pick is a grand idea for novice flower growers IF their location is good and if they don't mind staying home most of the time during the cutting season. If you wanted to try a U-Pick in your own home flower garden, you would have to worry about several things: the neighbors complaining about car traffic, whether foot traffic in your own garden could do a lot of damage, zoning laws and increased insurance costs.

I also think a U-Pick might not be a good idea at all if there were any other such U-Pick flower fields in the area. I live in an area where there are numerous U-Pick strawberry fields in the summer, but I feel that's quite different. Strawberries are a short summer crop with a tremendous following: everyone, it seems, wants strawberries in June. But too much competition in U-Pick flower fields could make everyone lose—even the customers—if the flower growers went broke.

The Grandees live just outside a large city and so can draw on many people. Their local environment is completely rural and very scenic, in sharp contrast to the urban and industrial areas nearby. These assets seem especially important to me in their success—along with their hard work and determination to keep at it. A U-Pick flower field carries the admonition given to most small retail businesses: pay attention to location, location, location, for that can be the most important key to success. If you have a field in a just-right location, give a U-Pick a try.

SNAP SEEDS IN
THE TUNDRA

I wanted to interview flower growers Rick Kaminskis and Annely Germaine of Dayton, Oregon, for several reasons—the primary one being that they began their cut flower business while living in Alaska. I couldn't visit growers in every section of the country while writing this book, but surely people who had taken up commercial flower raising while living in Alaska could offer an example and encouragement to people in all weather zones of the country.

Their little farm in Dayton was very sunny and warm on the day we met, but over delicious apple strudel, fresh local strawberries, and coffee, Annely and Rick recalled those first years in Alaska when, "for the fun of it," they threw out some snapdragon seeds and were amazed at the lush full stems that came up. They thought they were probably inspired in the effort by a long-ago article on small scale commercial flower growing in *Mother Earth News*. They are quiet, intelligent young people with wry, self deprecating humor that tends to hide the intensity of their gardening efforts.

They worked, met and married in Alaska (Annely

came there as an Austrian immigrant at the age of twelve), and in 1984 they moved forty miles out of Anchorage to the little town of Palmer. Their first commercial growing effort was a U-Pick strawberry field. They had plenty of customers (a four page waiting list) and got a good price ($1.25 per lb., U-Pick), but that still wasn't enough, they say, because of all the costs and hard work involved. They gave it up.

But their first casually grown crop of snapdragons were quite lovely and caused their friends to encourage them to take some to florist shops.

"They welcomed us with open arms,"said Annely. "Everything floral in Alaska comes at great expense and poor quality—by air."

They had no idea what to charge that first year ("and really gave the flowers away," adds Rick), but eventually got a copy of a wholesale marketing report which was published in Seattle, and from that they decided to bring their prices up to at least match those in Seattle.

They grew snapdragons and other flowers both in poly tunnels and outside. The season in Alaska is incredibly short, beginning in late May or early June and lasting only until Labor Day. They got little sleep in the summer time.

Rick quit his job in 1986 and stayed home with a new baby, Brendon, now 7, while Annely continued commuting the forty miles each way to Anchorage where she worked as an advocate for the disabled in the civil rights division of the Alaska state government.

Winters in Alaska they read and re-read the seed catalogs and picked out new flowers to try each spring. Besides snapdragons, they successfully grew and sold salvia, lavatera, and spider asters ("those grew better in Alaska than they do here.") They grew the seeds in potting soil ("because we didn't have the foresight to bring in buckets of soil to thaw") under a grow light in a spare room. Their Alaska flower growing efforts never took up more than a quarter acre, but from the beginning, "flower growing has always been our favorite way to work hard and earn very little extra money."

I've always easily understood why people leave Alaska, but I sometimes wonder what keeps them there year after year.

"Alaska," Annely remarked, "has a mystique that kind of grabs and holds you. I think it's a kind of a macho thing. Maybe that only the tough can handle it? And the land there is sooo beautiful. There was Pioneer Peak, always covered with snow, almost in our front yard. And the few people living there give one a sense of freedom. It's an illusion, of course, because you are really a slave to other things: the oil company, the wood stove." Sometimes it would take her over two hours to drive the forty miles to work, with people in the ditch every hundred yards or so.

After her parents left Alaska to return to Austria, Annely and Rick decided to move south. They brought their flower growing habits and ambitions with them and began to look for a small farm where they could raise their two children (Heather is now 2). They settled on forty acres along the Yamhill River halfway between Highway 5 and the Oregon Coast.

Twenty-five of those acres are leased out for corn raising, eight of them are river swamp-land, and the couple now works very hard on a couple of the remaining acres to raise perfect flowers for the Oregon market. Their primary crop is still snapdragons, the lushest and most delicately colored blossoms imaginable.

They put the starts in greenhouses long before spring

and take them to market before anyone else can provide such outstanding snaps. Besides making certain that they grow them very early, they have also learned just which colors the florists will love—perhaps before the florists realize it themselves. It's this kind of attention to details that makes for success in a small flower growing business: knowing exactly how early you can put something in an unheated greenhouse bed and have it grow well and fast, and knowing where the flower markets are heading as far as colors and styles are concerned.

Snapdragons are also quite difficult to ship so that they retain their full, rounded blossom stems, so very well grown local ones can often bring a premium price—especially those that come in a little early. Their favorite snap strains for growing right now are Potomac, Supreme, Oregon, Apache, Philadelphia and Michigan, among others. They grow only single stem varieties as those come on much quicker and have "less chance of gathering bugs and disease." After harvesting they also strip the stems of leaves.

Rick and Annely spent their first couple of years in Oregon driving into Portland a few mornings a week to the Oregon Growers Market, getting acquainted with the Oregon florist trade and making connections in the area. The OGM is a flower growers co-op on Swan Island in the Willamette River near Portland. Florists come there on Monday, Wednesday, and Friday mornings all year to see what's available from growers in the area. Membership is approximately $3,000 and that allows growers to rent space in the market whenever they need to show their wares.

Rick and Annely have not used the market very much lately as they've found a floral route business that very much appreciates their flower production, so now they usually deliver just to that one business two or three times a week. Their flowers are then carried to flower shops along the route by this flower wholesaler. And he pays the couple cash each time they deliver to him. Rick says he thinks he delivers about a thousand bunches of snaps a season, ten stems to the bunch. And he also guesses that they could sell twice as many as they are growing now.

But snapdragons are not the only blossoms they grow. In fact, it's obvious that they try new varieties every year in a fairly intensive search for something unusual that florists will want: something pretty, long lasting, easy to use, and not too expensive.

Just now in one greenhouse they are about to harvest a thick hedge of *Trachelium:* airy sprays of tiny star-like blossoms on tall stems, faintly aromatic, delicately elegant. They found it in their winter seed catalog search. It's lovely and unusual; I'm certain every florist in the Pacific Northwest would be delighted to have some.

And outside are rows and rows of zinnias, statice, delphiniums (for next year), lupines (all the blossoms already cut and sold), poppies, snapdragons (for late deliveries) and, their newest interest: silver king artemisias and santolinas for some wreath making. For reference, they use the Ball Red Book, a grower's guide put out by the Ball Seed Co.

This effort is not a super easy one. They still water everything by hand, hoping someday to install an irrigation system with water from the river. Right now they have to be very careful with the well water usage, in order not to overtax it. There is also a lot of grit in the water lines which sometimes creates even more problems.

The water quality where they live is so bad that they must purchase distilled water to use in flower harvesting. The local water has a bad pH, and is too high in both iron and silt. The first time they put cut snap-dragons into it, the stems collapsed within hours.

Like every greenhouse grower, they are driven crazy by insects late in the season. "Aphids are born pregnant," says Annely, as if to explain to herself the incredible aphid blooms she sees in the greenhouses as they warm up in late spring. They have to spray once a week in the greenhouses.

This last year they grew 28 different varieties of flowers, made money on seven or eight of them, and must consider the rest as simply more steps in this long learning experience that began years ago in Alaska. Annely still works off the farm to make ends meet. They are still not certain they can ever make a good living by flower growing alone. But they are hooked on trying and have a very good living in so many other ways that I must consider them quite successful.

Their kitchen window looks out on huge walnut and elm trees, the children play in the fields with a seemingly endless supply of cats. Rick is becoming active with the school board and they've found the rural area to be very supportive of schools and full of good neighbors. They have what many of the growers I've met have and enjoy in the life they've chosen: a way to live out of the city and the suburbs, to live the simpler life offered in small towns and rural areas, and to be able to bring up their children in a seemingly saner, more old fashioned way.

GARDEN FLOWERS FOR
ALL OCCASIONS

Their business card says it all: "Floral Hill, Garden Flow-ers For All Occasions." Think about that last phrase for a moment and you can probably see into one of the key ideas behind this book and the whole concept of growing a flower business at home. One primary difference be-tween a home based floral business and, say, a florist shop, is in the extended idea of "garden flowers" vs. commercial flowers from a flower shop.

George and Fanny Carroll of Eugene, Oregon, use that business card and are a perfect example of the garden flower approach. But before introducing them to you, I'd like to touch a little more on these contrasting ideas of floral businesses.

Surely every reader of this book is familiar with what is commonly available from ordinary florist shops, and more especially from flower delivery services anywhere in the country. You choose a floral arrangement from a picture on one side of the country, pay an ample fee, and that identical bowl of flowers is delivered to your Aunt Betsy's hospital room on the other side of the country a few hours later. And I mean the identical bouquet. The arrangement is usually a mound shape of bright, fairly long lasting flowers, most probably chrysanthemums or carnations. And, candidly speaking, it somehow looks like it was made in a flower factory. That's what you might call *traditional* flowers or florist flowers.

Now, pick up any current home and garden magazine and look at the bouquets featured in the recent stories of the English Country or French Country or just plain Country style of home decorating. Lots of flowers you never see in most flower shops—flowers you see only in the gardens of real gardeners. Or maybe in your grandmother's garden: columbines, foxglove, hollyhocks, Sweet Williams, lavaterra, cosmos, pincushion flowers, bleeding hearts—the list is almost endless. These are what I mean by *garden* flowers.

It is my contention, and that of many other knowledgeable people, that the flower market in America, and around the world, is moving strongly in the direction of these *garden* flowers and away from the long popular but more *traditional* florist flowers. This movement in the flower market is very good for small, home based, creative flower growers and sellers. And this movement is very obvious in the Carroll story that follows.

George Carroll is a biology professor at the University of Oregon. His wife, Fanny, is a trained pharmacist who has learned that she much prefers pushing flowers to pushing drugs. They run a fairly large commercial flower operation from their home garden in Eugene by selling bouquets at the Eugene Saturday Market, and garden flowers for many other occasions. They mostly run the flower business in the summertime—"so George doesn't have to teach summer school"—and were into their eleventh year of the Saturday Market when I visited their garden recently.

The farmer's market in Eugene has been going strong for many years and there is much competition there in the cut flower business. Yet over the years the Carrolls have gained a following of people who not only buy flowers from them regularly, but also ask the Carrolls to supply flowers for the special events in their lives: weddings, graduations, anniversaries, birthdays, and bar mitzvahs.

George probably started the whole thing years ago when he decided to take some of his own grafted fruit trees to the Saturday Market to sell. As the Carrolls grew scads of flowers even then, George thought it would be a great idea if his young daughters, ages 10 and 12, went along to sell a few flowers and learn a little business sense by taking responsibility for making change and tending to a small flower stand. The girls took in thirty to fifty dollars per Saturday and the demand for the garden flowers seemed quite strong. But the young girls soon lost interest, took up dance classes and other more important activities on Saturdays, and Fanny came on to replace them. She became caught up in the market herself, sensing the potential in growing unusual flowers and turning them into dramatic arrangements.

Over the years the Carrolls have developed some rules of thumb that guide them in their growing.

Rule #1. "We grow what we like."

Rule #2. "We grow unusual things every year. So we don't get bored."

Rule #3. "We make certain each new type we grow will hold up as a cut flower."

They swear by two seed catalogs: Thompson and Morgan and Park Seeds. (See the reference section for addresses.) They think that these two seed houses have rich enough floral offerings to keep them occupied and interested for years to come.

The Carrolls grow 95% of their plants from seeds and George tends to these in a little shed of a greenhouse where he makes his own soil mix for starts, keeps the seed beds warm with heating cables underneath them, and keeps a milk-house heater handy for the occasional dramatic drop in temperature that can occur in this otherwise mild climate zone.

Their garden lot is about one acre with a sloping terraced garden facing southwest. The property is fenced but there is no possible easy way to keep out the invaders from all sides: quack grass, rumex, blackberry vines, and rampant morning glory. George sprays with an herbicide at the end of every season and covers the annual beds with thick stacks of newspaper, but every spring the invasion from all sides begins again. They weed endlessly, mulch, and sometimes, to keep from spraying during the growing season, will use a brush to paint Roundup® on invading morning glory vines.

The Carrolls took a year off on sabbatical recently and went to Japan. On my visit they had just finished the months of garden clean-up required after their long sojourn and, to me, the garden looked nearly perfect—although the weed problems just over the fence were pretty scary.

They begin at the market each year on Mother's Day weekend. And to get ready for each Saturday, Fanny prepares about ten to twenty buckets of preserving solution on Thursday evening and begins picking flowers early Friday morning. She makes her own preservative

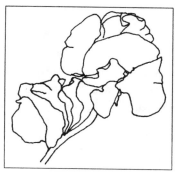

Sweet pea

adding 1/4 cup of sugar and 1 teaspoon of bleach to each gallon of water.

She uses some favorite Japanese scissors for cutting and picks much of the morning and evening on Friday, waiting to pick sweet peas, for instance, until Friday evening so as to keep them especially fresh. Her sweet pea stems have three blossoms and she picks them when the bottom two blossoms are fully open and the top one closed. It will open quickly.

For the Shirley poppies, she picks and throws away everything in full bloom on Friday evening and then picks the buds showing color early Saturday morning. She ties two dozen poppies together and, in her kitchen, puts the stem ends in boiling water for one minute. (See the section on harvesting and conditioning.)

On Friday evening, they arrange half of the flowers in bouquets and leave the rest in buckets to be arranged at the market. The next morning they back up their Toyota Tercel to the porch where they've left everything overnight, and put all the flower buckets in the back end of the car. On really big days they have to make two or three trips to get everything.

Typically, they will have one bucket filled with small four dollar bouquets, one bucket with five dollar bunches, and one with those for six dollars. Plus a few big ones. They have sold bouquets for as high as twenty dollars at the market but that is rare. More often they will offer twelve and sixteen dollar bouquets along with the less expensive ones.

Their steady customers tend to buy a ten or twelve dollar bouquet plus a six or eight dollar one, "or an eight and a four", says Fanny. These people know the flowers will last them all week, and they'll be back again the next Saturday to decorate their homes with fresh garden flower bouquets all over again.

When I asked her to describe an eighteen or twenty dollar bouquet, Fanny said it would contain perhaps six light blue delphiniums, six dark blue ones, five or six big white peonies, three magenta ones, plus some sweet William and tall ribbon grass. That sounded more like a fifty dollar bouquet to me, but both George and Fanny say that they feel a lot of competition at the market and that they must keep their prices as reasonable as possible to keep their business as good as it is. Even at that, they are the most expensive bouquet sellers at the market.

They keep lots of wet newspapers at the stand, wrapping every bouquet with a rubber band, then into wet newspaper and then they place all in a recycled plastic bag. They also offer a little packet of Floralife™ with each bouquet. They almost never sell flowers by the stem, although other people do so at the market.

Fanny is French, with the gestures and style of a woman who knows how to work very hard and turn out things that look very, very beautiful. She seems to combine a practical approach ("I know just how many poppies it takes to make a certain look in a bouquet") with a flair for the dramatic that obviously makes people open up their eyes and their purses and buy those bouquets.

I asked them to describe how a good day would finish up at the market and she said, "We would take in two hundred dollars and get home by noon." George's version was "We take in five hundred dollars and work hard until 4:30 in the afternoon." Over the years they've had many Saturdays of each kind.

When asked to describe a bad day, they both moan and say, "Fifty dollars and then we're stuck with all the flowers." Does that happen often, I wonder? "Only when there are big competing events in the community—and we've learned now just when those are, so we don't over cut on those days." And what happened to all those flowers on a bad day? "I just drove all over town," says Fanny, "and presented my friends with their choice of bouquets. By the time I was finished with that they'd made me feel like Lady Bountiful and I was feeling good again about the world." Overall, for the season, they think they probably have to waste 20% of what they cut for market.

They are both confident that their good success as bouquet sellers at the market is due to the fact that they offer unusual flowers and have a real knack for arranging them dramatically. They have learned just how much to cut to end up with a balance at the market so they can make fine bouquets all day long. For greenery they use: sword ferns, a variety of herbs, ornamental grasses, *Epimedium*, ladies mantle, ribbon grass, yarrow and *Artemisia*, "plus anything else that looks good."

The Carrolls also sell a few starts in the market as George has become so adept at raising plants from seeds. Typically, he sells a four inch pot of alstroemeria for $2.50. The other floral enterprise these two very bright,

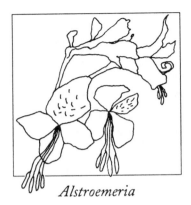

Alstroemeria

hard working people have developed is a summer wedding flower business that takes as much work (or more) than the Saturday market—although George and Fanny see the two as entirely complementary.

They never advertise for business, and only recently had their little business cards printed. But over the years, by word of mouth, they have built up an almost weekly wedding business—sometimes with two or more in one weekend, and have managed to make it all come out quite profitably.

First of all, Fanny says, she gives one free hour of advice and consultation to all wedding clients. But after that she charges twenty dollars per hour. She tells them on their first inquiry to do their homework so that they can keep their costs down.

"What are you going to wear? How many in the party? Who is going to wear boutonnieres? Who is going to wear corsages? Where is the reception? What do you want displayed at the church? At the reception?"

Surprisingly, Fanny doesn't have a book of photos to show her clients, but says she probably should put one together one of these days.

Rose corsage

George and Fanny have a friend who is a caterer and who loves to incorporate flowers in her food as decoration. She will recommend the Carrolls as wedding florists when she sees that they match up well with the wedding family.

"The wedding business is a lot of work," says Fanny, "and it should be a work of art and a work of love. So you don't want to do it for people you simply don't like. It becomes just too unpleasant." Because they have all the business they can handle, she trusts her own judgement in the first conversation with people about weddings and, when she feels she may not like them very well, she simply tells them she can't take on the work that weekend.

Or if there is any haggling about money she turns down the job. Fanny knows very well that she is giving good value and, to her, money haggling just means the job is not worth doing. She also feels she has to turn down any job with conflicting style differences: if the people are very, very formal, she knows her own more open, dramatic style would not be appropriate.

She describes a wedding to me that she will be doing

the following weekend: Five bridesmaids' bouquets. A wreath and a bouquet for the bride. Seven boutonnieres. Seven corsages. A very large bouquet for the entrance to the church and another large one in the sanctuary that can be carried to the reception hall. An herb bouquet and a garland for the bar and another garland for the hall. Plus sixteen small table centerpieces. Price for all that? $350.00. Sounds like a real bargain to me.

Fanny has taught herself to make the wedding floral specialities, and on one or two occasions has traded flowers for a lesson or two from a florist. "The important thing is that I've learned to do these little decorative things (like a headband or a boutonniere) very, very quickly," she says.

How can they get all the work done in time for all the ceremonies? They sometimes have to have helpers or even enlist wedding family members to help. This is where Fanny's practical, by the numbers, methods come in handy. "I tell them to start with twelve stems of ladies mantle and eighteen stems of Sweet William and after that to add anything they want to to make it their own."

George's approach is very different. "He arranges everything just by his feelings," says Fanny.

"What's amazing, though," answers George, "is that we always come within a dollar or so of each other in pricing a bouquet. We just start out differently."

Sometimes, for weddings, they have to buy a few things from wholesale florists and Fanny also keeps an eye on a local discount florist's ads in the paper and can now and then pick up some real bargains she can use with her own flowers. They do buy baby's breath and ferns when their own garden is out of them and, of course, white roses or anything that special wanted by the bride or family.

Besides weddings, the Carrolls also supply flowers for special dinner parties or luncheons, graduations, and wedding anniversaries, and many other special occasions. Fanny often asks her special occasion customers to bring her the vases and tell her where they go in the house so she can do the designs to match the container and the space.

The Carrolls have no desire whatsoever to own or operate a florist shop. They love the freedom their home business gives them (the chance to go to Japan for a year, for instance.) And they use the money from their florist ventures to pay for all their garden equipment and expenses ("including good tools from Smith and Hawken") and to buy special vases they may want. Most of all they use it to bolster their income when it is cut off in the summer time.

They have purchased very little for the flower business. They don't use a refrigerator, and do all their work on cleared off kitchen counters, dining room tables, and an adjoining laundry room.

Besides the two seed catalogs they order from, they use a basic *Sunset Western Garden Book* , the multi-volume *New Illustrated Encyclopedia of Gardening,* edited by T. H. Everett, and one old, probably out-of-print reference book, *Flowering Plants of the World,* edited by V.H. Heywood.

The plants they grow are so numerous that I will just list them now and say that they are all worth trying by any cut flower gardener because they are recommended by Fanny and George Carroll, garden flower growers *extraordinaire.*

CARROLLS' PLANT LIST

Acidanthera
Adenophora
Agapanthus
Ageratum
Alchemilla mollis
Alstroemeria
Althea rosea
Amaranthus caudatus
Ammi majus
Amsonia
Aquilegia
Artemisia
Asters
Astilbe
Astrantia
Bletilla
Bupleurum
Bupthalmum
Campanula
Centaurea
Coreopsis
Corn Cockle
Cosmos
Cotoneaster
Crambe
Crocosmia
Delphinium
Epimedium
Eremurus
Erigeron
Eupatorium
Feverfew

Gaura
Gladiolus (Perennial only)
Gomphrena
Gypsophila
Helenium
Helianthus
Heliopsis
Japanese Anemone
Lavatera
Liatris
Ligularia
Lychnis
Lysimachia
Lythrum
Marguerites
Michaelmas Daisies
Mints
Monarda
Monbretia
Monkshood
New England Asters
Nicotiana
Ornamental Grasses
Painted Daisies
Phlox
Physostegia
Platycodon
Pride of London
Ribbon Grass
Roses
Salvias
Scabiosa

Liatris

Shasta Daisies
Shirley Poppies
Snapdragons
Stachys lanata
Statice
Sunflower
Sweet Peas
Sweet William

Sword Ferns
Tassel flower
Thalictrum
Trachymene
Verbena
Veronica
Yarrow
Zinnia

BETTER BLOSSOMS
WITH BRAIN POWER

Now let's take a look at a flower operation that is small but so well thought out, efficient, and profitable that it can probably only be explained by the background and character of the growers.

John and Frances Chadwick ran a flower shop in Redondo Beach, California, for many years. A big flower shop with 25 employees, huge walk-in coolers, and as many as 15 to 20 weddings to do on busy weekends in June.

After 25 years they sold the shop and retired to a life of leisure and travel, pulling a travel trailer back and forth across the U.S., Canada, Mexico, and Central America. Back and forth and back again for years until they'd suddenly had enough of all that and decided to *really* retire. This time into nearly full-time flower growing at home.

The Chadwicks live on less than an acre of ground in Rainbow, California—a tiny little shady spot off old Highway 395 near Fallbrook. Their modest home is comfortable and welcoming, full of interesting mementos from their travels and John's finely crafted handmade furniture. Some of the furniture definitely belongs in a crafts museum.

A shady patio extends out the rear of the house and just now it's filled with the odor of sweet peas from a thick bank of multi-colored blossoms in the tiny back yard. Beyond that are the greenhouses where John and Frances, without any hired help whatsoever, do a steady booming business by growing gerbera daisies (*Gerbera jamesonii*) and stephanotis blossoms (*Stephanotis floribunda*) for florists all around the Southern California area and well beyond.

If you don't know the gerbera, you haven't been to a flower shop in a long, long time. They have become the florist's choice all over the country and the world because they are long lasting, tall stemmed, and outstandingly beautiful. One or two gerberas turn an ordinary bouquet into an arrangement. Gerberas are native to South Africa (are sometimes called Transvaal Daisies) and have been turned by Dutch flower masters into a nearly perfect hybrid wanted by flower merchants the world over. Today's gerberas will produce flowers twelve months a year (when grown with proper care at the right temperature) and produce many blossoms in a small space.

John Chadwick first grew gerbera daisies from seed as a young high school student. Nowadays he grows them by the thousands with a careful, knowledgeable approach that leaves little to chance. The Chadwicks do not heat their greenhouses so their gerbera flower stem production drops off considerably in the winter and gives them some welcome time off.

But their gerbera return is certainly worthwhile by almost any standard of calculation. Each and every flower stem brings them thirty five cents. Anytime, all the time. And in less than six thousand square feet of greenhouse space they produce up to fifteen hundred stems per week, every week, except for a few during the winter.

Frances and John handle all the labor themselves, seemingly with ease. They certainly don't give the impression of over-worked, over-stressed people. The physical work seems to suit them (both are slim, healthful looking seniors) and the brain power they've put into the operation is quite obvious, even to a casual observer.

Over a few beds of gerberas is a little trellis system where the Chadwicks grow stephanotis blossoms—one of the most desirable of all wedding flowers. The blossom is a white, waxy little flower that smells of orange blossoms, Polynesia and lovely wedding bouquets. Florists buy them in small clear plastic boxes for about 50 cents per blossom and then have to wire every single blossom with a wire stem and fit them into the wedding boutonniere or bridal bouquet.

Stephanotis blossoms grow on an evergreen vine and produce a profusion of blooms in the Chadwick greenhouses between May and October. The trellis system uses ordinary white string tied above the waist-high trellis so that the blossom stems can run up a couple of feet above Frances Chadwick's head when she does the picking of the flower clusters onto cookie trays. Then the blossoms are put into the clear plastic boxes and placed in a cooler until taken to the wholesale flower house the following morning. John bought a small walk-in cooler ("at a very good price") from a nearby McDonald's when the restaurant switched to a bigger cooler. Stephanotis blossoms can't drink water once they've been picked, so they must be kept cold and taken to market very quickly. The Chadwicks get fifteen cents for each tiny white flower, and each cluster usually holds up to six flowers.

꘎

One fascinating aspect of the flower business is that multi-national companies are involved in it all over the world and yet it can be done quite successfully by individuals in a simple, almost neighborhood fashion. It is a business that can be operated from a backyard flower garden yet often includes high-tech, scientific methods. The Chadwicks run a small, backyard operation, but their business definitely reflects these other, more complicated aspects of the world cut flower market.

These days they buy their gerbera starts from a company called Max-i-Mum, in Carpenteria, California. That company gets the starts originally as tissue culture plantlets from the parent company, Terra Nigra, in Holland.

Tissue culture is a system that turns certain specific plant cells, taken from a desirable plant, into a clone of that plant when the cells are grown in nutrient solution in a test tube. It offers relatively fast, relatively inexpensive mass production of tiny plantlets that turn into perfect replicas of the parent plant.

The first plants to be grown this way commercially were orchids in the 1960s. Since then the method has been used successfully in many applications including the growing of carnations, roses, phlox, rhododendrons, kalmia, lilies, and, of course, *Gerbera jamesonii*, grown by the Chadwicks.[2]

When the Chadwicks order a group of gerbera starts from the company in Carpenteria, they order a specific variety by name: i.e., *Estelle* or *Merci*. Other plant growers all over the world are ordering that specific plant by that name and will receive an identical plant—a clone. A newsletter from the company keeps the Chadwicks informed of new varieties, their stem length, production per plant per year and any new colors available. Right now the color cerise is a best seller and the Chadwicks also keep trying to get a perfect yellow gerbera on a nice tall stem.

"If they don't produce the way we want them to ," says Frances, "then out they come. And in go the new ones to try."

The soil in the beds is a sandy loam with added redwood shavings plus lime and super phosphate, as recommended by the gerbera experts. The water and fertilizer formula is also recommended by experts and runs on a simple automated system that allows John more time for other parts of the operation. It's these inputs of expertise, science, and international know-how that allow the Chadwicks to run this intensive operation without any hired help and with a relaxed, time-to-spare attitude that makes it seem like they are having a wonderful time.

John is responsible for picking the gerberas and shows his visitors how to recognize the very first sign of maturity in the flower head, so that it can be picked the first day it is ripe and not earlier or later. The flower center shows a thin line of yellow pollen at the outer edge of the center, closest to the petals. The flower should be picked when that line of pollen first appears. When picked at the perfect stage, he explains, the flower will last the longest and yet will require no chemicals in the water except a bit of chlorine bleach to kill any bacteria. No nutrients or preservatives are required because the flower blossom is fully mature and will last up to two weeks if picked at this perfect time.

He picks each stem with a twist near the base of the plant and then cuts across it at a slant with clippers. This allows the stem to drink the water and not lie flat against the bottom of the bucket, unable to take up water. He cuts a bucket full of flowers, placing each stem immediately in cool water with a tablespoon of bleach to the gallon of water. The buckets are then taken to a small shop area near the greenhouses where the packing takes place. John pushes a little wax paper cup up along each stem so that it cups the flower head to hold and protect it. He then places ten of these protected stems in a cellophane sleeve to give protection to the entire bunch.

The buckets are then placed in the cooler overnight and twice a week they are delivered to a wholesaler who then distributes to flower shops around most of Southern California. Once a week a floral route man also picks up at the Chadwick home. This delivery/wholesale service provides John with the flower cups to protect the flower heads, and they are the ones who pay him the set price for the gerbera stems, day in and day out. They will take every flower he can provide and very much appreciate the high quality product the Chadwicks are offering. They even buy John's smaller flowers, or those with shorter stems, for a slightly lower price.

Everything about the operation is careful, yet somehow casual; exacting and yet done with a relaxed approach that probably comes from so many years of learning how to do everything just right. I'm struck by the ability of these people to deal in one of the biggest, most important flower crops in the world and to be able to find a niche in it. It's easy to imagine how many giant companies must be in the gerbera growing business. Yet here are the Chadwicks in tiny Rainbow, California, growing exactly the number of flowers they want to grow and finding a fine, reliable, well paying market that just goes on and on.

"We give them the quality they want," says John, "and they seem happy to have our crop."

Freshness and care in handling add days and days to the life of cut flowers. Millions of flowers are shipped into this country every day from other countries (dry-shipped at cold temperatures) and most flowers take several days and a lot of rehydration and chemical additives before ending up on the buffets and dining room tables of customers around the country. Drooping gerbera stems and other appearance flaws are a common problem for florists everywhere and a costly problem to deal with. The Chadwicks have a system that prevents those kinds of problems and allows them to do very well as small growers in competition with very big growers.

Their growing is not entirely problem free. Both plants have some serious bug problems which require almost weekly spraying with toxic chemicals. Both plants need constant, daily picking to keep the quality just right. So traveling is out of the question these days. But they had years and years of that, says Frances. And now they both seem completely content, laughing at the little flower prison they've built for themselves.

They now use some of the proceeds from their floral operation to help keep their granddaughter in college. And they recently bought their grandson a fourteen hundred dollar clarinet to play in his high school band. In his "spare time", John is building a computer table for his granddaughter's dormitory room.

---

[2] For those readers interested in learning more about the tissue culture of plants, please see the bibliography at the back of the book.

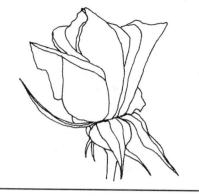

WEALTH AMONG
THE WEEDS

Around the Portland flower markets, one name comes up repeatedly. Dave Clark.

"You've got to talk to Dave Clark. Crazy Dave Clark."

"If you really want to talk to someone who knows about small growers, you should talk to Dave Clark."

"The guy who knows all the latest stuff and what everyone is trying is Dave Clark."

A build-up like that is irresistible to me. I had to find him. And that turned out to be easy. Dave runs a small business called Portland Wholesale Florist, has a little space at the Oregon Growers Market in Portland, and was on the phone laughing when I found him there one Wednesday morning. Laughter is a constant with Dave—he uses it like verbal punctuation, and at least half of it is always directed at himself. Dave Clark also considers *himself* a bit of a crazy but, of all the growers I've met, he is probably the most innovative, the most resourceful—certainly the most humorous.

And, as a small grower myself, I felt especially drawn to Dave because he said that if I could *"stand a lot of weeds"* he'd meet me at his little farm, thirty-five miles south of Portland. I'm embarrassed about my own weed problems so often that I immediately recognized a soulmate in Dave Clark. Of course I can stand a lot of weeds. And do—every day. I drove happily down to Aurora, where Dave met me at a truck stop and led me to his five acre patch at the end of a long lane.

Dave's weeds are awesome. But he has a fine excuse for them. Last fall he underwent open heart surgery for a life threatening heart condition that had gradually turned him into an invalid. For someone who has been growing plants and raising flowers out of doors since the age of five, becoming an invalid must have been a grim experience.

But his operation was a success and Dave's health is almost perfect again. In the meantime, the weeds and gophers stormed in while he was away and now he is facing a major overhaul of much of what he had accomplished before. But he's so naturally optimistic (and glad to be alive) that he seems almost undaunted by the work ahead.

Clark is still fairly young, well built, a little on the short side. He keeps his hair cut very short and his laughter going almost non-stop. His property is only 135' wide but runs a quarter mile deep. A small barn, a little greenhouse, a few pieces of equipment, and almost every other square inch of the five acres is covered with plants. And weeds.

The weeds themselves are pretty impressive at first glance, but once we start the show and tell of the plants, I am far more impressed with the work and thought and creativity that has gone into this unusual operation.

Many cut flower businesses are for the season, with not too much thought about the seasons to follow. After all, fashions and fads in flowers can and do change. New colors, new species, new decorating ideas—who knows what will be popular years from now? For most of us, it is enough to plan and think a little about the next growing season. We tend to put garden and mind to rest in the fall until the new seed catalogs come in the middle of winter to reawaken our dormant flower thoughts.

For Dave, the whole idea of a floral business is working toward a future where he can beat the game of always dealing with fresh flowers going rapidly stale, and the constant replanting necessary to keep up with a fresh flower market. His goals are to be able to successfully dry much of what he grows, or else to be able to cut his profits off trees and shrubs that require almost no maintenance and grow on their own, more or less forever.

"There's so much dumpage in the fresh flower market," says Clark. "Maybe up to 50% at times. I'm trying to go at it another way."

His latest effort towards *another way* is the recent purchase of a freeze-drying machine that he uses to dry roses, other flowers, and even vegetables, which he can then use in arrangements and wreaths.

Freeze drying machines, Dave reminds me, were developed by the American Red Cross in World War II for the freeze-dried storage of blood. And, he adds, they were used by the Smithsonian for their wildlife exhibits—which sometimes meant the freeze-drying of whole animals.

Dave's machine has a 3' x 5' cylinder that can hold up to three thousand roses at a time. When it's turned on, the temperature drops to 60° below freezing, and a vacuum pump turns the ice to gas and literally sucks all the moisture out of the flowers.

Most flowers are air dried and we all buy and appreciate flowers which have been hung to dry in barns. But that kind of drying tends to wither and fade the flowers, leaving them wrinkled and somewhat discolored. The freeze drying of flowers leaves them far fresher looking: the tiny rosebuds Dave shows me are smooth as can be and delicately colored. They look altogether different from the rosebuds I dry at home.

He paid twelve thousand dollars for the machine, but says that if new it would have cost twice that. Dave keeps the machine in a room at his parents' barn, thirty five miles away. One of his primary floral products is freeze-dried rosebuds at fifteen dollars per dozen. For these he has been growing thousands of unusual small roses (called x-plants) that he purchases from Jackson and Perkins at $1.95 to $2.25 per plant. "You can see how quickly I can pay for these plants with just two or three buds." It costs about sixty dollars in electricity every time he uses the machine.

The sad part of this tale is that the horrible winter of '90-'91 brought a catastrophic below zero storm that took out many of Dave's special roses—along with so many other plants for growers all over the northwest. Now Clark is in the process of rebuilding his rose inventory, and has just replanted some of his favorites. He calls out the names as we walk the field: "Here's the little Mercedes, the only rose that will dry as a true red. And look, here's 'Porcelana,' and the lovely Eloquence. These dry to perfection."

The other things Dave has planted seem even more interesting to me and full of potential profits. One of the most valued greens for wreaths at Christmas time is the Western white pine, with its silvery green foliage. Dave has put in a thousand of these along one side of his property and they are already taller than he is and will soon be ready to pick. He also has another thousand of them planted at his parents' house and believes that in five more years each of these trees will produce up to ten pounds of perfect Christmas greens which should be going for at least a dollar a pound by that time. "I know," he says, "that I can make a good ten thousand dollars per year on just these trees in a few more years. The white pine is a native in the Pacific Northwest and becoming more and more scarce as the forests are cut down."

He has five hundred flowering quince shrubs that are still small but growing quite well, even though right now they are closely surrounded by weeds. He has installed overhead sprinklers and has an excellent well that, in the hot summer months, can keep everything watered as much as necessary.

He grows incense cedar and eucalyptus *gunni* for wreaths. The low lying part of the land (which holds a lot of water in the winter) is planted in twisted willows (*Salix matsudana Tortuosa*) and fantail willows (*S. sachalinensis Sekka*), both heavily used by florists.

Dave does grow more ordinary flowers for his wreaths and arrangements: zinnias, acrolinium, xeranthemum, nigella, and others. But it's the long term plantings he has done that make his place look so very productive, despite all the weeds.

Oregon offers small farmers a special tax break with Exclusive Farm Use (EFU) zoning. That means people like Dave pay the lowest land taxes in the state: $298 per year for his five acres. He only needs to produce two thousand dollars per year on it to keep that farm status.

Dave studied cut flower production and floral tissue

culture at Cal Poly University in San Luis Obispo, California. He has worked in many flower shops, even owning three of his own at one time, but prefers the freedom of doing his own field flower production nowadays. He still works occasionally for other shops, does design work on floats in the Rose Parade in Portland, floral arrangements for parties, or a half dozen other floral jobs to keep the wolf from the door. He started in the flower business as a delivery boy in Southern California and believes that "once you are in the flower business you never, ever get out of it."

Besides the plants on the five acres in Aurora, Clark is also growing some unusual tropicals from South Africa and Australia on his brother's acreage in Brookings, Oregon: kangaroo paws, protea, and green calla lilies.

He feels that the American flower market is stuck on a plateau right now until flower marketing breaks through to a new level. It's got to get more like Europe, he believes, with people able to buy flowers everywhere all the time. Only then, he believes, will flowers really take off in this country. He decries the efforts he has seen in many communities to take flower stands off the street corners. But he also feels that more mass marketing people will be taking up flowers soon and retailing them in the biggest retail stores in the country.

He thinks the wreath market is coming back even stronger than before and that dried flowers will once again equal or surpass the current popularity of silk flowers. His present slogan is: "If you can't dry it, don't try it."

Dave is one of the few small growers I've met whose earnings come only from the flower business. And to do it, he is a jack-of-all-arts, super-experienced, somersault artist who can land on his feet in any situation and clip and snip his way to the bank. If he can hang in for a few more years, I feel strongly that he will do very, very well.

Meanwhile, he is looking for a couple of tons of old newspapers to use as mulch in his new plan for weed control. "What on earth will all these gophers think of that?" he muses, shaking his head in laughter.

GAMBLING ON
FLOWERS

Inside a warehouse in San Marcos, California, is a good place to take a look at one level of flower marketing that some small growers have been able to plug into. There are lots of walk-in coolers, long work tables covered only by shed roofs, and buckets and buckets of flowers everywhere you look. Several men are packing flowers into huge florist boxes that will travel immediately by truck or air to flower shippers up and down the west coast and to other wholesalers around the country. Everyone is moving quickly; phones ringing, trucks and cars in and out, an obvious reflection of an awareness that this product is *alive* and needs to be moved very fast.

Don Manor is a flower broker. He deals directly with growers, about eighty of them, in both San Diego County and across the border in Mexico. Some are very big growers, some very small. It's the small ones that interest us and that I've come to talk to him about.

For Don, the most important issue between the grower and the broker (who is really the grower's salesman) is not size. It's cooperation, trust, and the ability of each to see the other's problems.

Don is also a part time grower, so he can appreciate the problems growers have. But his background and obvious talent are in marketing. For Don, today's flower marketing, even for the smallest of growers, takes place in the context of a worldwide market. Most of his sales are in the U.S., but the price of what he's selling is very often determined by what is coming into the U.S. every day from other countries such as Colombia, Japan, Mexico, Holland, and Israel, among others.

For those readers who might be interested in moving into a larger growing operation, I think it's of some value to take a moment here to look a little bit at that worldwide aspect of flower growing and selling. Then we'll come back to Don Manor and his recommendations to small growers.

For those who have traveled to Canada, Europe, and Japan it will come as no surprise that the U.S. is not number one in flower consumption. It seems that every other person on the streets of Paris, or Amsterdam, is carrying a bouquet. Even the tiniest store in British Columbia, Canada, sells potted flowers and bouquets. In Japan, the strong custom of gift giving keeps flower buying a very big part of the culture there. But, until recently, flowers have been very much of a *special event* purchase in America. And here, flowers have been sold almost exclusively in florist shops. That's a big problem, says Don, as florists are, by nature, quite conservative and unwilling or unable to change and push the flower market in the direction he believes it must get going. That's why the big increase in flower marketing, he says, is happening in supermarkets—where the truly aggressive marketing takes place in this country.

In the last few years things have begun to change dramatically and, according to a recent study in *FLO-*

RIST magazine, an FTD publication, flower purchasing is increasing so much every year in the U.S. that now there are predictions that America will move to the top of the list in flower consumption in the next ten to twenty years. Some of the reasons for this are primarily demographic: an aging population and a population that is moving more and more into the cities. Another reason our flower consumption will continue to increase is because more and different flower outlets are opening up. But for right now, Americans only purchase half the number of fresh cut flowers (on a per capita basis) that consumers in Japan or Europe purchase.

At the same time, and perhaps more importantly for small growers, many of the flowers we do sell come in from other countries. Nowadays we import most of our roses, chrysanthemums, carnations, pompon mums, gladioli, and many other types of blossoms. And several free-trade agreements in the offing will probably make our flower importation figures higher and higher. Land in Mexico, for instance, is much cheaper than land in America, labor is much cheaper there, and there's plenty of sunshine and good weather year 'round. At this writing, the U.S. and Mexico are negotiating a free-trade agreement that could possibly turn Mexico into the flower producing capital of the world. Japan now holds that position, with Italy as number two, followed by the Netherlands, with the U.S. in the number four position. Mexico right now has position number five in world flower production.

So what has all this to do with your little planned field of statice or the mixed bouquets you might take to market? Probably not too much until and unless you consider taking up flower growing in a much bigger way. And the moment you do that you must consider where all the new flowers you are growing can be sold. That step can put you very much into the world flower market depending, of course, on what, where, and when you want to grow.

When new growers in the Southern California area contact Don Manor these days, he tells them that unless they are growing something entirely new (to the market) and very unusual, they should perhaps wait a year or so until some problems specific to California are solved: the water problem, the economy (which was soft at the time of our visit), and the free-trade agreement with Mexico. He also tells them that they shouldn't plant anything without knowing how. Many previous citrus and avocado growers are now trying to get into flower growing, he says, and many of them don't have any idea what they're doing.

But his general advice to experienced small growers runs like this:

"If you want to be part of the larger market, talk to a broker or wholesaler first, to see if what you plan is really needed. Sometimes they can encourage you, for instance, into a quick few rows of Queen Anne's lace that can come to market just in time for Mother's Day, or an eight week crop of larkspur that can come on line just when it's needed.

"And please remember," he adds, "if you ask to know the price of a crop from a broker on one day and your plants don't come to market until much later, the price is liable to be much, much lower. The prices on most flowers change almost daily and depend very much on what's coming into the country, and what's growing in all the local fields. The successful small growers I handle are usually very, very good at one or two items and also have a good understanding of my problems. Sometimes I need

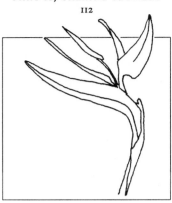

Streletzia (Bird of Paradise)

them to hold the flowers in the field for a day or two—to cut only when needed. A day or two in this business can make a big difference.

"The smart, small growers around here are turning right now to more difficult, long term crops that most people don't want to take the time to get into—something that takes an effort and some patience—while they're waiting out these uncertainties."

Along these lines, Don is putting in some varieties of bird of paradise plants (*Strelitzia*) for himself right now for the long haul. They can take up to five years to produce well, cost some money to get into, and require a little special care along the way.

"But later on my kids can harvest them for sale if they care to," he says, "because the plants last a long, long time, and the better florists always want them."

Don agrees that there is a real opening for small growers in the kind of neighborhood marketing we've been discussing in the other parts of this book. But he gives firm warning to any flower growers about coming into the business with big expectations and too naive an attitude about what a hardball world is out there in almost any business—especially one with the life span of a flower blossom. "I don't go to Las Vegas," he says. "I deal in flowers instead."

He also warns about unscrupulous brokers who promise one price to the grower, take the flowers to sell, and then later pay the grower a much lower price. "Check out any broker before you deal with him. Talk to growers who have dealt with him. Does the broker pay what he says he will and when he says he will? I pay weekly. Every week," he says, with enough obvious pride to make you realize non-payment or low payment is probably a fairly common problem in this business—at least in his area.

We've stopped near some buckets of an unusual flower that demands admiration and comment. It's called Baronia, says Don, and proceeds to tell the tale of this outstanding blossom that originated in Australia but may be subject to a plant virus that could soon cause its debut in the American flower market to be cut quite short—unless or until tissue culturists can solve the problem and bring it into the market in a big way.

It's well after noon by now. Don has been at it since 4 a.m. and he's a long way from being finished for the day. The men are still boxing flowers, the buckets of flowers are still everywhere and needing to be dealt with. I'm certain he knows lots more about this business but I'm starting to feel guilty about keeping him so long from his *gambling*. Adios, Don, and a million thanks for your time.

WHEELS OF
(GROWERS') FORTUNE

I first became interested in flower auctions on a trip to Holland a few years ago. The largest flower auction in the world is held there in Aalsmeer, outside of Amsterdam, in one of the largest buildings in the world.

Overhead catwalks allow visitors to walk about freely and look down to view what's being shown and sold in this incredibly large operation. The actual auctions take place in separate, glass enclosed rooms with huge price clocks that spin incessantly as hundreds of flower buyers from all over Europe gather and compete for the flowers, which are grown both in Europe and around the world. The flowers are brought in by truck to one end of the building and put on multi-shelved trolley carts. These are soon attached to tracks in the floor that automatically pull the trolley carts into one auction room or another where they are bid on and purchased by the seated buyers using electronic communication with the auctioneers. If you ever go to the Netherlands, I urge you to make a visit to the flower auction house at Aalsmeer. It's a sight you won't soon forget.

One of the few auction houses in North America

built to operate just like the one in the Netherlands is near Vancouver, British Columbia. I visited there a year ago when my friend Pat Brash went to purchase some flowers for her shop. This time I sat in on the auction itself and came to realize what a boon the auctions are for flower growers. In fact, it is the grower cooperatives who put these expensive operations together because they have learned just how much they can sell in an auction situation.

It's one thing to bring your flowers into a big warehouse and let buyers come from all over the region to take a look at them and pick out what they want to buy. It's quite another thing entirely to put all those buyers together in a room like a steeply raised auditorium and put two huge auction clocks overhead in front of them. It's very much as though the florists wanting to purchase flowers or green plants are invited to play a game in which masses of flowers are brought by for them to purchase. But the purchases must be made electronically, and always in competition with a few hundred other buyers who are all looking at the identical flowers. The buyers are asked to punch a button at their seat when they see something they like at a clock price they want. Instantly! The decision must be made in a split second.

There are three hundred florists and flower buyers watching those same flowers and plants and they all have their own buttons to press. The clock begins its swing at a starting price determined by the grower and all the buyers sit there staring intently at the clock with their fingers over the buttons, getting ready to hit that button at the instant the clock reaches the price they are hoping to pay. If they hit the button first, they get the lot of flowers at that price.

As the auction proceeds, an auction worker briefly

holds up a bucket or box or bunch of flowers of the type that are being bid on, the clock begins its swing and a few seconds later the batch is sold and the worker is holding up the next example to be sold.

Usually the flowers come through in groups or lots, so that if you don't get the flowers you want on the first attempt there are probably several more similar batches coming through for which you can try again. And again. Each lot of flowers that comes through the hall on the trolley sells at a slightly different price. All the buyers are competing with each other on each batch to get the very best price. And the prices may vary by only a few pennies for the same type of flower. But, for the growers, these auctions offer an excellent means to maintain prices and still give the buyers some sense of control in what they are purchasing.

The auction house opens at 4:30 in the morning so that buyers can arrive early and look over the plants and flowers in the warehouse. Each trolley of flowers is marked with the grower's name, the starting price and the amount of flowers in each lot. The auction itself starts at 6 A.M. and moves so fast once it begins that this early preparation is often essential for buyers—especially inexperienced ones.

Although the auction set up itself resembles a big game show, the action is quite serious with growers in attendance to see that everything is run according to the rules. The buyers and growers have little rituals they go through to keep the house in order. When an inexperienced buyer punched the button at too high a price for tulips, for instance, the other buyers in the hall booed, trying to impress on the buyer not to make that mistake again. When the price for a large lot of iris dropped too

Aster (Michaelmas daisy)

low, the growers pulled them from the auction rather than let them be sold too cheaply.

The most impressive thing about the auction is the tremendous quantity of flowers and potted plants that can be moved through the selling process in a very short time. There are two clocks going at the same time in the hall: one for flowers, the other for potted plants. Experienced buyers not only bid on both clocks at the same time, the electronic key pad at each seat also allows buyers to purchase for several shops at a time. Each sale often takes less than ten or fifteen seconds, and a computer system allows each sale to be recorded and the flower trolleys themselves marked with each buyer's name.

At the end of the auction, Pat and I walked through to the cashier's window where she paid for her purchases (the invoice had been prepared automatically once she made the purchases through the key pad), and then we walked back to the warehouse and found her order clearly marked and set aside for her. The auction is a remarkably well organized effort that serves both buyer and seller, but I must admit the advantage is to the seller. I'm

certain the growers do much better through the flower
auction than they could ever do without it. The competition among the buyers in the hall obviously helped keep
the prices up.

One florist sitting next to me nearly swooned as
several buckets of sweet peas came into the hall on the
trolley. "I can never get my hands on those," she said,
preparing to hit the electric key pad the second the sweet
peas were presented. She tried hard to purchase them but
lost out to a large florist who bought them all instantly.
Even here, I thought, it's the old fashioned flowers that
seem rare and desirable.

The auction usually runs until about 10 A.M. and goes
on two to five times per week, depending on the season
and the availability of flowers and plants. If you should be
in the Vancouver area sometime and don't mind getting
up early, you are welcome there as a visitor. Although not
as large as the one in Holland, this auction is very much
worth seeing. The address and phone number are: United
Flower Growers Co-Op Association, 4085 Marine Way,
Burnaby, B.C. V5J 5E2, tel. 604-430-2211.

I also attended an auction in Carlsbad, California
(long a flower growing mecca in that state but now much
more given over to real estate development). The
Carlsbad auction is a small one, run without a clock
through the use of a video screen. It lacks the drama and
excitement of the ones in Holland and in Vancouver, but
it's still worth seeing. In fact, I would again encourage
anyone who is really interested in selling flowers to visit
all of the florist warehouses and brokers or auctions in
their area, to learn all they can about what's going on in
the region. Many areas have buyer cooperatives and they
usually have warehouse space near other wholesale flo-

rists. Newcomers are most welcome to come and find out about membership costs and privileges.

The best place to start looking for such entities is in the yellow pages of any fairly large city near you. Look under wholesale florists and pay a morning visit to the places that are listed and you will quickly find out what is going on in your area in the wholesale flower market. Ask any wholesale florist if there is a grower's co-op in the area and pay them a visit, too. Don't worry that you may be too small to consider such a thing. I have been quite amazed to find out just how many small growers are involved in selling fresh cut flowers.

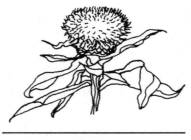

HOW THE PROS
DO IT

I thought it would be interesting to take a look, toward the end of this book, at a professional grower who has been in the business for quite awhile; one who has had some real success at it and also some very hard bumps along the way. Meet Paul Troutman and his wife Alison, owners and operators of Cascade Cuts, a small farm in Whatcom County near Bellingham, Washington, close to the Canadian border. I think their experiences as growers speak to what is the very best in this world of growing for market, and to some of the very worst that can await those who choose flower growing for a living.

Paul has a strong background in horticulture, having taken a degree in plant pathology at the University of Georgia, working all the while at nurseries while attending school. After graduation, he moved to the west coast to take a job with a large nursery near Bellingham. Following that job he hired on as a greenhouse builder and learned all he could about that part of the business. Soon after he met and married Alison Kutz, who was growing *Sempervivums* and was just taking up what was to become a long, involved, serious interest in the growing of herbs.

At about this time—in the early '80s—Paul read an article about freesia growing written by a professor at the University of Minnesota. He was intrigued enough with what he read to write to the professor asking for more information, thinking he'd like very much to learn to grow these lovely, fragrant blossoms. Freesias are both beautiful and bountiful, producing up to thirty stems per square foot.

The professor wrote back saying that he knew of only three suppliers of freesia bulbs: one in England, one in Holland, and one in Germany. More intrigued than ever, and sensing a possible opportunity, Paul wrote to the suppliers and learned that there were two freesia growers on the west coast, one in California and one only a few miles away in Langley, British Columbia.

Paul called the Langley grower, George, and said he'd love to buy some freesia bulbs and grow them for Mother's Day. Fine, said George, he could sell Paul some bulbs, but there were two stipulations: the bulbs needed a heat treatment right away in order to be grown successfully, and he, George, was leaving immediately for Holland.

Paul and Alison rushed up the highway to Langley and got the bulbs and some hurried instructions from the grower. They bought 24,000 bulbs—enough to plant 2,000 square feet of land. The problem was, they didn't have any land. At the time they were living with friends, looking at property and not having any luck at all in finding a place to rent that had a little land with it. But they bought the bulbs anyway and intensified their search for a place to rent. It took a month but they finally found a little farm east of Bellingham, where they still work and live.

They got the freesias in, and both took full time jobs in the area and worked in the evenings and long into the night to get their flower business going. When the freesias began to bloom, Paul would get up at 3 A.M. to deliver flowers to Seattle, a hundred miles away, and be back in time to start work at his job at eight o'clock.

Their first crop of freesias was a decent success and they used all they earned on that to make a down payment on the farm. They also ended up with 60,000 freesia bulbs that had multiplied from their first crop. They grew some delphiniums that were easily sold, and bought and installed their first greenhouse. They imagined that they could do a year 'round business in freesias which had become instantly popular and in great demand in the American flower market.

But their own inexperience and the real world moved in on them rather quickly. First of all, they fumigated the soil in the greenhouse with methyl bromide and did it at the wrong temperature so that the fumigation was a total waste. That meant that they had to weed over and over again that first year. The second year they brought in a lot of mushroom manure recommended by a grower in Canada and it was much too fresh and therefore too high in salts. Their freesia quality suffered immediately. At the same time, Canadian growers went heavily into freesias, which they promptly brought to the American market. An acre of freesias, says Paul, is an enormous amount of flowers that can, and did, change the market overnight.

Paul and Alison had to dump twelve thousand dollars worth of product that year which they felt wasn't good enough to take to market, and they could see that the Canadians were putting lots more resources into their freesia growing and would be very difficult to compete with. The Canadians had glass greenhouses, supplemental lighting, automated shading, and even thermal blankets for their soil.

The auction in Vancouver opened up at about the same time and their future in cut flowers began to look very bleak indeed. At first, says Paul, the auction seemed to serve small mom and pop nurseries and growers, but over the years he has watched very big European and Canadian corporate growers (even huge forestry companies) moving into the Vancouver auction and it has affected the whole northwest Washington growing scene. Oregon flower growers, he says, don't even ship to Washington any more because of the impact of the Canadian auction. Paul could become a member of the auction if he wanted to, but has chosen to try to find a more independent route.

During all this difficult time Alison went further and further with her interest in herbs and, with some intelligent selling methods, such as allowing small lot purchases of unusual herbs, and some energetic sales efforts, over the years they have become the pre-eminent potted herb suppliers in the northwest. In fact, the herbs now account for nearly a third of their business.

Paul continued with the cut flower business, growing both indoors and out, but always concentrating the growing on about an acre of ground. The farm now houses several greenhouses along with some outside fields where they have just finished growing several flowers for field trials for the University of Georgia.

His primary cut flower now is greenhouse forced snapdragons. He produces three hundred bunches of them a week on incredible stems of four to six foot lengths. They use a little plastic grid net over the beds that holds the tall stems up straight and keeps them from falling into each other. I had never seen such tall stemmed varieties, but there is a very special market in this country for extra tall stems of flowers used mostly in large, dramatic arrangements for hotels, restaurants and other public buildings and occasions. Paul sells his snaps to a wholesaler in Seattle who caters to that market.

Couldn't the Canadians come in now, I wondered, with extra long-stemmed snaps and cause the same problem all over again? Of course, says Paul, but so far there has been no sign of it. If it happens, they would just have to move into something else. After all, that's really what they have been doing all along, says Paul, except for the herbs. Always trying something new, always knowing that whatever they get into they may have to get out of it in a year or two as too many people follow them into the market.

It took Paul and Alison two or three years to realize that if they ever wanted to make a real living growing flowers, and not just knock themselves out after working all day at other jobs, that they would have to hire some help and get much bigger—not in space, but in production. That they have done. They have been in business now for almost eleven years and employ between 15 and 25 people, depending on the season. This year they will turn a staggering $650,000 on their growing—all on just a little over an acre of production, indoors and out.

Although they have had to learn some very hard lessons, they have also learned how to turn on the smarts. They now clean their soil with steam, eliminating both the need for herbicides and crop rotation. They bought a low pressure steam boiler, and use quick-connect aluminium pipes that they can set up anywhere on the farm. They attach a perforated pipe down the center of a tilled bed and turn on the steam under a tarp and steam blanket. In four to five hours, it builds up enough steam heat to kill off all the weed seeds.

For insect control, they are using primarily biological controls, bringing in beneficial insects to control aphids and other common greenhouse pests. When necessary they use Safer soap plus a very new organic spray made from the neem tree. "We want to live here a long time," says Paul, "and be able to drink the water while we're here."

The labor problems most growers complain of so often don't bother Paul and Alison. Their helpers seem to be very much their neighbors.

"We have really good people," says Paul. "We even get a lot of older people, a lot of very bright people. They sometimes come here when their lives are a little bit in crisis and they are looking for something different. It's often like a sanctuary for them to be near all the greenery."

The farm has a special feeling of hard work and good humor about it. People are both laughing and working hard every place you look. The Troutmans seem to give people lots of responsibility, yet there is obviously a very supportive environment on the farm, both for plants and people. If I were looking for work, I think I'd go there.

The outlook for the flower and plant business is excellent, says Paul. Their own business has just taken another 30% leap in sales. He believes that at least the outdoor and bedding plant business is virtually recession proof. "When people have to stay home more, they take more interest in their homes."

They sell to nurseries, garden centers, and grocery stores. Alison did all the selling the first three years, calling on all the accounts and getting acquainted. Now in the spring time the phone rings off the hook and they have to make far fewer sales calls. Besides the herbs and cut flowers they also sell bedding plants, hanging baskets, and ivy geraniums. They have about twenty thousand square feet under cover and ten to fifteen thousand square feet in outdoor production.

Paul's latest endeavors are in the potted bulb business—growing lots of unusual bulbs, like chinodoxa, anemone blandas, unusual crocus varieties, and many others as indoor flowering house plants. At the time of our interview, he had some 300,000 bulbs coming in from Holland. He was also on his way to see the banker as the business is so big now that he must incur a lot of debt in the winter to grow what he will sell in the spring—to pay off the winter's debt.

Looking far down the road, Paul sees that groundwater laws will become tougher and tougher. Eventually they may even have to get into total water recycling. The cost of energy continues to go up—he paid a thirty thousand dollar fuel bill last year and ran up nearly two thirds of that in a six week period during last winter's two horrendous storms. At my visit he was having natural gas installed throughout the farm.

Last winter's storms also made him realize just how risky this plant business can be. And probably just how much he has learned in the last few years. They were without power for seventy hours. Their water and diesel lines froze. Sheets of ice formed on the greenhouses as the northeasters came through, ripping off a furnace stack and a layer of plastic from one of the greenhouses. Paul climbed up to cut off the damaged stack and fell sixteen feet through another greenhouse roof into one of the beds. They just started to recover from that mess and their generator blew a rod and had to be replaced, at twelve thousand dollars.

They have no crop insurance; it is far too expensive. So their crop insurance is their maintenance man, their attentive employees, and their own intense daily concern and care.

Even with all the horror stories, Paul does see a good market out there for people interested in working hard in the cut flower business. He thinks seasonal outdoor production would be a good way for a grower to go, but it would have to be on a fairly large scale in order to work out financially. He believes there is a very big market for delphiniums grown very, very tall on thick stems, like his snaps. "They don't ship well either," he says, "and I don't see too many of them coming in from Canada." And he says repeatedly how very much better flowers look and sell when they are sold close to where they are grown. "The local grower's biggest advantage is that his product isn't stuffed in a box."

I couldn't agree more.

PART III

THE CUT FLOWER CATALOG

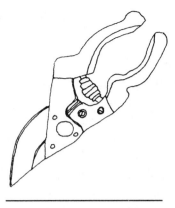

CUT FLOWER
CATALOG

LIST OF LISTS

Now comes the naming of names, the pointing and praising, the list of lists. First of all, a list of perennial plants I recommend for anyone who chooses to try a business in bouquets. Of course, it's not complete. How could it be, with new flowers being tamed and brought in from the wild every day, with hybrids being hybridized by many people everywhere, and with some parts of the floral world still not catalogued.

The first perennial list is a good beginning for beginners. It's all the perennials that I have tried myself, that I can give some growing and conditioning details on, and can list with some assurance that you'll find them saleable as cut flowers.

My own growing is fairly limited so the second list is the Experts' Choice—all the other perennials that my reading and interviewing have taught me are good flowers for commercial use—either for bouquet selling or in small acreage lots to brokers or wholesalers, to flower shops, or at Saturday markets.

Then comes my list of annuals and biennials, those wonderful, forgiving plants that can make "fine gardeners" out of all of us, no matter what our limitations. These too are the ones I've grown myself and can give a few hints on. They will add to any bouquet garden and almost all are very easily grown. And that is followed by a list of the Experts' Choice in annuals and biennials.

Because I use "everything I can lay my hands on" in the art of bouquet making, I then offer lists of shrubs, vines, and trees, plus one of bulbs, corms, and tubers— many possibilities you may already be growing or want to grow to add to your cut flower business. Most are species I've found to be very helpful in creating bouquets. These lists too are followed by the Experts' Choices—other species and varieties that I have not grown much myself but that are recommended by others as having commercial possibilities. There is also a list of herbs that can be used for cut flowers, especially as greenery.

A list of flowers considered best for drying is offered last. I have found over and over that fresh-cut flower people are always trying dried flowers, often selling dried flowers right along with their fresh flowers, often learning to make items with dried flowers that they can market. Even though I don't give specific instructions for flower drying in this book (maybe in the next one?) I do think a list of possibilities is always helpful.

CUT FLOWER LISTS

GARDEN PERENNIALS
AUTHOR'S CHOICE

❀ *Achillea*

(Yarrow)   Zones 2–8

Flat clustered heads on tall stems in yellow, white, pink, red.

CULTURE
Very hardy. Needs sun; tolerates dry ground.

PROPAGATION
Seeds need 30 days or more at 60-65°. Divide plants in fall.

HARVEST AND CONDITIONING
Cut when heads are half open. Condition in cold water, removing bottom foliage.

BEST VARIETIES FOR CUTTING
A. millifolium: Fire King or Cerise Queen: *A. filipendula:* Coronation Gold or Gold Plate.

DRYING
Excellent flower for drying. Almost any variety. Hang to dry.

❀ *Aconitum*

(Monkshood)   Zones 2–7

Tall dramatic spikes of (usually) blue/purple flowers. Deeply cut leaves. Caution: all parts are poisonous if eaten.

CULTURE
Prefers partial shade and cool weather. Divide every 3-4 years.

PROPAGATION
Seed difficult to propagate. Find nursery stock.

HARVEST AND CONDITIONING
Cut when 1/2 of flowers on stem are open. Use warm water and preservative.

BEST VARIETIES FOR CUTTING
Try any variety available in your area.

DRYING
Not recommended.

❀ *Alchemilla*

(Lady's Mantle)　　Zones 3–9

Lovely lobed leaves with tall stems of tiny greenish flowers. Good for filler and bouquet greenery.

CULTURE
Sun or partial shade. Self sows easily.

PROPAGATION
Easily grown from seeds or divisions.

HARVEST AND CONDITIONING
Cut when flowers first open. Warm water and preservative.

BEST VARIETIES FOR CUTTING
A. mollis

DRYING
Hang to dry. Recommended.

❀ *Alstroemeria*

(Peruvian Lily)　　Zones 7–10

Small, exotically colored lily-like blossoms on tall stems. Mainstay of florist industry.

CULTURE
Likes partial shade, good drainage, and no disturbance once planted.

PROPAGATION
Only freshest seeds germinate. Easier to purchase nursery stock. Will spread and self-seed.

HARVEST AND CONDITIONING
Cut when 3 or 4 flowers open. Very sensitive to ethylene. Use warm water and preservative.

BEST VARIETIES FOR CUTTING
Ligtu hybrids.

DRYING
Not recommended.

❀ *Anemone*

(Japanese anemone) Zones 5–8

Tall stems with saucer shaped flowers in pink or white on a green mound of grape-like leaves. Blooms late summer.

CULTURE
Needs fairly rich, well drained soil. Partial shade.

PROPAGATION
Can be grown from seed. Usually grown from nursery starts.

HARVEST AND CONDITIONING
Cut when buds show full color. Warm water and preservative.

BEST VARIETIES FOR CUTTING
Try any Japanese anemone available in your area.

DRYING
Not recommended.

❀ *Aquilegia*

(Columbine)　　Zones 3–8

Spurred, airy flowers on long stems with a few delicate leaves. Perfect for bouquets.

CULTURE
Partial shade to full sun (in mild climates). Needs good drainage but otherwise easily grown.

PROPAGATION
Seeds require 1-3 mos. at 65°-75°. Starts usually available and plants will self-seed.

HARVEST AND CONDITIONING
Cut when blossoms are more

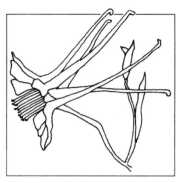

Aquilegia (Columbine)

than half open. Remove all lower foliage. Condition in warm water and preservative.

BEST VARIETIES FOR CUTTING
Try any variety over 15" tall, e.g., *A. caerulea, A. canadensis, A. formosa, A. chrysantha.*

DRYING
Seed pods can be air dried.

❀ *Armeria*
(Thrift or Sea Pink) Zones 3–10
Low mounds of thick greenery. Tall stems of single globular flowers. White to pink and red.

CULTURE
Likes full sun and good drainage. Good coastal plant. Fine edging plant.

PROPAGATION
Seeds, starts, and fall divisions.

HARVEST AND CONDITIONING
Cut when blossom shows full color. Treat with warm water and preservative.

BEST VARIETIES FOR CUTTING
A. pseudoarmeria has longest stems. Sometimes sold as *A. formosa.*

DRYING
Hang to air dry. Related to statice and drys well.

❀ *Aster*
(Michaelmas daisies) Zones 4–9
Fall garden mainstays. They form small hedges of thick colorful blossoms in blues, pinks, white, or purples with (mostly) yellow centers.

CULTURE
Easily grown, but can get mildew. Don't wet foliage. Needs dividing every two years.

PROPAGATION
These don't come true from seeds. Get nursery starts which can be divided every year.

HARVEST AND CONDITIONING
Cut when most of a flower cluster is open. Foliage wilts quickly, so remove after cutting. Split stems. Use warm water and preservative.

BEST VARIETIES FOR CUTTING
There really are hundreds of varieties. *A. novae-angliae* and *A. novi-belgi* are the most common species, but try any that claim growth over 18".

DRYING
Not recommended.

❁ *Astilbe*

(Formerly called Spirea.) Zones 4–8

Medium tall plumes of airy blossoms: white, pink, or red. Attractive foliage.

CULTURE

Prefers moist, cool location. Partial shade.

PROPAGATION

Get nursery starts and divide every third year.

HARVEST AND CONDITIONING

Cut when flower plume is almost entirely open. Split stems. Use warm water and preservative.

Best Varieties for Cutting: *A. arendsii, A. chinensis, A. tacqueti.* Plus try any variety sold locally that claims growth over 15".

DRYING

Can be air dried, but silica is recommended.

❁ *Campanula*

(Bellflower)   Zones 3–10

"Cup and Saucer Plant" in the old fashioned garden; an amazing array of varieties offering tall spikes of purple, white, and blue blossoms.

CULTURE

Easy care in sun to partial shade. They do attract slugs and snails.

PROPAGATION

Easy from seeds, starts, divisions, and cuttings.

HARVEST AND CONDITIONING

Cut when flowers are almost open. Burn stem ends with flame for 15-20 seconds. Use warm water and preservative.

BEST VARIETIES FOR CUTTING

C. carpatica, C. glomerata, C. lactiflora, C. rotundifolia.

DRYING

Not recommended.

❁ *Centaurea*

(Knapweed)   Zones 3–9

Nice, bushy plants producing excellent cut flowers in three distinct varieties. (See below.)

CULTURE

Easily grown in sun. Divide every three years.

PROPAGATION

Simple from seeds, starts or divisions.

HARVEST AND CONDITIONING

Cut when flowers first open. Use warm water and preservative.

BEST VARIETIES FOR CUTTING

C. dealbata , John Coutts, rose colored flowers. *C. macrocephala,* yellow hardhead or globe centaurea, bold, thistle-like blossom. *C. montana* mountainbluet or perennial cornflower, fine blue filler flower. *Montana* can be invasive.

DRYING

Only *C. macrocephala* is recommended to dry as a flower. Others can be dried as a *calyx* (after petals and seeds have dropped).

❀ *Centranthus*
(Red Valerian. Jupiter's Beard)
Zones 4–10

Slightly bushy plant with conical clustered flowers in white, pink, or red. Great filler flower. Fragrant.

CULTURE
Needs sun, but prefers cool summers. Can be cut back for second bloom.

PROPAGATION
Easily grown from seeds, starts, divisions, or cuttings.

HARVEST AND CONDITIONING
Cut flowers when clusters are 1/4 to 1/2 open. Split stems. Use warm water and preservative.

BEST VARIETIES FOR CUTTING
C. ruber, C. albus, C. roseus.

DRYING
Not recommended.

❀ *Chrysanthemum*
(Mums)   Zones 4 or 5–10

Very large genus, but "mums" are usually upright, bushy plants with 3" or 4" blossoms. Many colors.

CULTURE
Need sun. For better blooms, pinch back main stem when plants are 6" to 8" high. Divide every year or two.

PROPAGATION
Easy by seeds, starts, divisions, and cuttings.

HARVEST AND CONDITIONING
Cut when flowers are open but centers still tight. Remove foliage below water level. Warm water and preservative. Can last a long time.

BEST VARIETIES FOR CUTTING
C. arcticum, C. coreanum, C. morifolium, C. nipponicum. Other important varieties: **Shasta Daisy,** *C. maximum.* Truly indispensable garden bouquet flower. Easily grown, needs dividing every 2-3 years. Many fine forms including Alaska Esther Read and others. **Painted Daisy,** *C. coccineum,* also called *Pyrethrum.* Excellent cutting flower in shades of pink and red.

DRYING
C. parthenium (Feverfew) is good for drying.

❀ *Cimicifuga*
(Bugbane)   Zones 3–10

Stately spires of white stamens (the petals drop off) create a fluffy floral plume.

CULTURE
Partial shade is best, but give lots of water if grown in full sun.

PROPAGATION
Buy seeds or spring divisions.

HARVEST AND CONDITIONING
Cut when flower stem is half open. Use warm water and preservative and add a little bleach to the water if the odor seems too strong.

BEST VARIETIES FOR CUTTING
C. racemosa, C. simplex. Or try any variety available in your area.

DRYING
Not recommended.

❀ *Coreopsis*

(Tickseed) Zones 4–10
Abundant stems of bright yellow daisy-like flowers, 18"-24" tall.

CULTURE
Very easy plant. Likes full sun and will bloom more if you pick spent flowers.

PROPAGATION
Seeds or spring divisions.

HARVEST AND CONDITIONING
Cut when flower is fully open but center tight. Long lasting. Use warm water and preservative.

BEST VARIETIES FOR CUTTING
C. grandiflora, C. verticillata, C. lanceolata.

DRYING
Not recommended.

❀ *Delphinium*

(Perennial Larkspur) Zones 3–10
Tall, lovely favorites for every serious gardener who can grow them. Usually blue blossoms, although white, purple, and even red and yellow are available in some areas.

CULTURE
Often need staking, fertilizer, thinning, lots of water, and cool summers. They are attacked by snails and slugs, lots of pests and diseases. They can be quite troublesome, but they are so beautiful.

PROPAGATION
Seeds take 14 days in 50-55°. Also grown from basal cuttings taken in spring.

HARVEST AND CONDITIONING
Cut when 1/2 of the flowers on a stem are open. Prick stem with a needle just below the flower head (to keep out air bubbles) and fill stem with water, then plug stem with cotton or floral foam. Condition in cold water with preservative.

BEST VARIETIES FOR CUTTING
Pacific hybrids and Blackmore and Langdon hybrids are considered the best and easiest to grow.

DRYING
Both delphiniums and the annual larkspur are recommended for drying.

❀ *Dianthus*

(Carnations, Cloves, Pinks)
Zones 3–10
Not the florist carnation (those are grown under glass), but fairly tall stemmed single and double blossoms from grey-green tufts of foliage.

CULTURE
Prefers slightly alkaline soil and cool summer weather. Divide every 2 or 3 years.

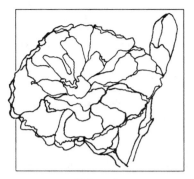

Dianthus

PROPAGATION

Can be grown from seed, but the best named varities must be propagated vegetatively.

HARVEST AND CONDITIONING

Cut when flowers are 3/4 open. Cut just above stem joint. Put in deep cold water with preservative.

BEST VARIETIES FOR CUTTING

Try any variety offered locally that claims growth over 15". For seeds, try *D. knappii* or *D. allwoodi*.

DRYING

Not recommended.

❀ Dicentra

(Bleeding Heart)   Zones 3–9

Ferny, graceful plants with arching stems of heart-shaped pink or white flowers.

CULTURE

These are fairly short-lived in warm winter climates; they prefer some shade and a well drained, humusy soil. Can be divided in early spring.

PROPAGATION

Seeds can be tricky, taking up to three months to germinate and must be frozen first. Best to buy nursery stock.

HARVEST AND CONDITIONING

Cut when 1/2 of the flowers are open on a stem. Leave as much foliage as possible on the plant. Condition in cold water with preservative.

BEST VARIETIES FOR CUTTING

All good for cutting. Try whatever will grow in your area.

DRYING

Not recommended.

❀ Dictamnus

(Gas Plant. Burning Bush)
Zones 2–9

Fragrant foliage with tall racemes of white, pink, or purplish flowers followed by attractive seed pods.

CULTURE

Rugged, easy-care plant. Don't divide or disturb.

PROPAGATION

Seed grown plants take a long time to flower. Find nursery stock wherever possible.

HARVEST AND CONDITIONING

Cut when flower stems are 1/3 open. Condition in cold water with preservative.

BEST VARIETIES FOR CUTTING

Try whatever is available.

DRYING
Seed pods make handsome dried flowers.

❀ *Doronicum*

(Leopard's Bane)   Zones 4–9
Bright yellow daisy flowers that bloom very early above low mounds of heart-shaped greens. They bloom with the tulips.

CULTURE
These do best in cool climates. They go dormant in summer. Easy to grow.

PROPAGATION
Seeds, starts, or divisions.

HARVEST AND CONDITIONING
Cut when first open and condition in warm water and preservative.

BEST VARIETIES FOR CUTTING
Caucasian Leopard's Bane.

DRYING
Can be dried in silica.

❀ *Echinacea purpurea*

(Purple Coneflower) Zones 3–10
Daisy-like, purplish flower with drooping rays and protruding center. Long bloom time.

CULTURE
Hardy, low maintenence plant that needs sun.

PROPAGATION
Easy from seeds, starts, and divisions.

Echinacea purpurea
(Purple Coneflower)

HARVEST AND CONDITIONING
Cut when flowers are open, center very tight. When petals drop, centers still look good in bouquets.

BEST VARIETIES FOR CUTTING
Bright Star, Robert Bloom, The King.

DRYING
Only the centers are recommended for drying.

❀ *Echinops*

(Globe Thistle)   Zones 3–10
Blue globes on tall stems with grey-green thistle like prickly leaves.

CULTURE
Needs sun, otherwise very easy.

PROPAGATION
Seeds or divisions.

HARVEST AND CONDITIONING
Cut when 1/4 of the globe is covered with open flowers. Split stems. Use warm water and preservative.

BEST VARIETIES FOR CUTTING
E. ritro or *E. humilis.*

DRYING
Excellent. Harvest *before* tiny flowers appear.

❀ *Eremurus*
(Foxtail Lily. Desert Candle)
Zone 5–9
Imposing spires of delicate flowers, they open from the bottom up.

CULTURE
Needs deep, rich, well drained soil.

PROPAGATION
Seeds much too slow to flower. Find nursery stock.

HARVEST AND CONDITIONING
Cut when 1/2 of the flowers on a stalk are open. Use warm water and preservative.

BEST VARIETIES FOR CUTTING
E. himalaicus, E. stenophyllus.

DRYING
Not recommended.

❀ *Eryngium*
(Sea Holly)   Zone 5–10
Interesting silver to blue bracts and cones; thistle-like foliage with stiff, tall stems.

CULTURE
Likes full sun. Not easily moved. Needs good drainage or dry soil.

PROPAGATION
Easily grown from seed.

HARVEST AND CONDITIONING
Cut when fully open. Treat with warm water and preservaive.

BEST VARIETIES FOR CUTTING
E. giganteum. Try any others you find.

DRYING
Used more for drying than as fresh.

❀ *Euphorbia*
(Spurge)   Zones 4–9
Two kinds are good for flower bouquets (see varieties). Both have milky sap that can be irritating to the skin.

CULTURE
Both kinds easily grown in light shade or full sun in cool climates.

PROPAGATION
Grow from seeds or divisions.

HARVEST AND CONDITIONING
Cut *polychroma* when clusters are half open, *corollata* when flowers are open. Burn stem ends with flame or boiling water. Treat both in warm water and preservative.

BEST VARIETIES FOR CUTTING
E. corollata, also known as Snow on the Mountain. Baby's breath, *E. polychroma,* blooms a lovely chartreuse green in early spring.

DRYING
Not recommended.

❀ *Filipendula*
(Meadowsweet)   Zones 2–9
Fluffy stems of pink or white tiny florets.

CULTURE

Prefers damp, even wet soils and partial shade.

PROPAGATION

Seeds or spring divisions.

HARVEST AND CONDITIONING

Cut when stem is 1/2 open. Condition in warm water and preservative.

BEST VARIETIES FOR CUTTING

F. rubra, F. purpurea, F. vulgaris.

DRYING

F. ulmaria is best for drying. Grows naturally over much of North America. Called "Queen of the Meadow."

❀ *Gaillardia*

(Blanket Flower)   Zones 3–10

Bright showy daisy with multi-colored rays: red, yellow, orange, or purple. Centers are dark and hairy.

CULTURE

Easy, dependable plant in sun. Prefers dry soil.

PROPAGATION

Seeds, starts, and divisions.

HARVEST AND CONDITIONING

Split stems. Cut when flowers open but centers still tight. Remove lower foliage. Use warm water and preservative.

BEST VARIETIES FOR CUTTING

G. grandiflora.

DRYING

Not recommended.

❀ *Geum*

(Avens)   Zones 5–10

Five frilly petals of orange, red, or yellow. Clumps of green leaflets.

CULTURE

Full sun or light shade. Can't take too much cold.

PROPAGATION

Seeds must be very fresh. Buy starts and divide later.

HARVEST AND CONDITIONING

Cut when flowers are 3/4 open. Condition in warm water and preservative.

BEST VARIETIES FOR CUTTING

Named varieties such as Mrs. Bradshaw, Starker's Magnificent, and Red Wings.

DRYING

Not recommended.

❀ *Gypsophila*

(Baby's Breath)   Zones 3–10

A billowy, bushy plant of tiny, airy white (or pink) flower sprays. The indispensable filler.

CULTURE

Needs lime (sometimes called "chalk plant"). Prefers full sun, and not being disturbed.

PROPAGATION

Seed or starts.

HARVEST AND CONDITIONING

Cut flowers when spray is 1/2 open. Condition in cold water.

BEST VARIETIES FOR CUTTING

G.*paniculata*, Bristol Fairy,

Perfecta, Pink Fairy.

DRYING
Excellent. Hang to dry.

❀ *Helenium*

(Sneezeweed)   Zones 3–10
Daisy-like flower heads in yellow, gold, and brownish purple.

CULTURE
Easily grown in full sun. Can stand wet soil.

PROPAGATION
Seeds. Plant divisions in spring.

HARVEST AND CONDITIONING
Cut when petals are open but center is still tight.

BEST VARIETIES FOR CUTTING
H. autumnale, Bruno, Butterpat, Brillant. Try any available locally.

DRYING
Not recommended.

❀ *Heliopsis*

(False Sunflower)   Zones 4–9
Zinnia-like daisy of bright golden yellow on tall stems. A little on the coarse side, but nice.

CULTURE
Tolerates poor dry soil. Divide every three years.

PROPAGATION
Seeds or buy named varieties. Can be divided in spring.

HARVEST AND CONDITIONING
Cut when flower first opens and center is tight. Treat with warm

water and preservative.

BEST VARIETIES FOR CUTTING
H. scabra, Gold Greenheart, Karat, Golden Plume, or others.

DRYING
Not recommended.

❀ *Heuchera*

(Coral Bells)   Zones 3–10
Clumps of leaves give rise to a whole bouquet of tall stems of graceful flower sprays.

CULTURE
Easily grown. Full sun or partial shade.

PROPAGATION
Seed or division.

HARVEST AND CONDITIONING
Cut when half the spray is open. Buds do not open in water. Treat with warm water and preservative.

BEST VARIETIES FOR CUTTING
H. sanguinea hybrids.

DRYING
Not recommended.

❀ *Hosta*

(Plantain Lily)   Zones 3–9
Usually grown just for lovely basal leaves, they also produce delicate flower spikes that last well in bouquets.

CULTURE
Need some shade and lots of moisture. Snails and slugs do love them.

PROPAGATION
Seeds take months to germinate

and extra care. Easier to buy plants to start. Can be divided.

HARVEST AND CONDITIONING
Cut when two or three bottom flowers are open. Split stems. Condition in warm water and preservative.

BEST VARIETIES FOR CUTTING
H. caerulea, H. fortunei, H. sieboldiana, and others.

DRYING
Not recommended.

❀ *Kniphofia*

(Red Hot Poker. Torch Lily. Tritoma) Zones 6–10

Tufted clumps of arching, strappy leaves with stout stalks of orange-red-yellow tiny flowers packed into the "poker tip".

CULTURE
Needs sun, good soil, and lots of moisture, plus good drainage.

PROPAGATION
Seeds. Purchase available hybrids.

HARVEST AND CONDITIONING
Cut when flower is half open. Split stem. Use warm water and preservative. Also nice cut as buds only.

BEST VARIETIES FOR CUTTING
Try any tall hybrid available in your area.

DRYING
Not recommended.

❀ *Liatris*

(Blazing Star. Gay Feather) Zones 3–10

Tufts of excellent white, pink, or purple flowers that open from the top of a tall spike over leafy mounds of green. Florist mainstay.

CULTURE
Needs full sun or partial shade. Well drained soil and sometimes needs staking.

PROPAGATION
Grow from seed or corms.

HARVEST AND CONDITIONING
Cut when flowers are half open. Split stems. Treat with warm water and preservative. Long lasting.

BEST VARIETIES FOR CUTTING
L. spicata, L. aspera, L. pycnostachya.

DRYING
All good for drying except for the white varieties.

❀ *Limonium*

(Sea Lavender) Zones 3–10

Large glossy leaves close to the ground, with stiff stems of tiny, airy, lavender blossoms. A perfect bouquet filler.

CULTURE
Needs full sun and prefers sandy soil. Drought tolerant.

PROPAGATION
Seeds are possible, but resultant plant slow to bloom. Best to try nursery stock.

HARVEST AND CONDITIONING
Cut when cluster is half open. Condition in cold water.

BEST VARIETIES FOR CUTTING
L.latifolium. L. tataricum, German statice (See annual listing for statice.)

DRYING
Excellent for air dryng.

❀ *Lupinus*

(Lupine) Zones 4–9
Tall spikes of often bi-colored, thickly clustered flowers. Attractive palmate leaves.

CULTURE
Grow in sun or light shade. Does best in cool climates. May need staking. Doesn't like being moved.

PROPAGATION
Seeds or nursery stock.

HARVEST AND CONDITIONING
Cut when 1/2 of the flowers on a stem are open. Prick stem with pin, fill with water and plug (see general instructions in Harvest and Conditioning).

BEST VARIETIES FOR CUTTING
Russell hybrids.

DRYING
Not recommended.

❀ *Lychnis chalcedonica*

(Maltese Cross) Zones 3–10
Tall, tall round heads of scarlet florets.

CULTURE
Full sun, well drained soil.

PROPAGATION
Easily grown from seed.

HARVEST AND CONDITIONING
Cut when flower heads half open. Split stems. Use warm water and preservative.

BEST VARIETIES FOR CUTTING
L.c. Plena.

DRYING
Not recommended.

❀ *Lychnis coronaria*

(Rose Campion) Zones 3–10
Bright cerise flowers growing on tall, woolly grey stems and leaves.

CULTURE
Does well in poor, dry soil. Reseeds itself.

PROPAGATION
Seeds.

Harvest and Conditioning: Cut when flowers are open. Use warm water and preservative.

BEST VARIETIES FOR CUTTING
Some confusion in these names, but almost any are worth trying.

DRYING
Not recommended.

❀ *Lysimachia*

(Loosestrife) Zones 3–10
Tall spikey flowers that are easy to grow and use in bouquets.

CULTURE
Like damp places. Spread, can be invasive.

PROPAGATION
Seeds or divisions.

HARVEST AND CONDITIONING
Cut when 1/2 of spike is open.

Condition in warm water and preservative.

BEST VARIETIES FOR CUTTING
L. clethroides, gooseneck loosestrife; *L. punctata*, yellow loosestrife.

DRYING
Good if dried in silica.

❊ *Malva*

(Mallow)   Zones 3–9
Resemble hollyhocks with small white or bright flowers on a columnar stem.

CULTURE
Easily grown in sun or partial shade. Self-seeds.

PROPAGATION
Seeds, plus transplants from self-seeding.

HARVEST AND CONDITIONING
Cut when blossoms first open. Condition in warm water and preservative.

BEST VARIETIES FOR CUTTING
M. alcea .

DRYING
Not recommended.

❊ *Paeonia*

(Peony)   Zones 2–8
Spectacular blossoms on clumps of handsome greenery. Singles and doubles. Some fragrant, some not.

CULTURE
Must be planted carefully so that growing tips (eyes) are not more than 2" below soil surface or they will not bloom. Needs slightly alkaline soil. Each planting clump needs 3 to 5 eyes. Needs sun or light shade and lots of water. Flower stems may need staking as buds and blossoms are heavy.

PROPAGATION
Seeds difficult but possible to grow.

HARVEST AND CONDITIONING
Leave at least three complete leaves below each stem cut. Cut when the color is showing but blossom is less than 1/2 open. Split stem ends. Condition in cold water.

BEST VARIETIES FOR CUTTING
Try any hybrids available in your area. All are fine for cutting.

DRYING
Can be air dried or in silica.

❊ *Papaver orientale*

(Oriental Poppy)   Zones 3–9
Large crepe like petals of brillant colors, often with dark splotchy centers. Dramatic, outstanding flowers grown on large, hairy clumps of grey-green foliage.

CULTURE
Easily grown where summers are cool. Leaves die off after bloom.

PROPAGATION
Buy named varieities. Some seeds available.

HARVEST AND CONDITIONING
Burn stem ends right after cutting for 15-20 seconds. Condition in cold water. Flowers only

last a few days even with treatment, but are worthwhile for very fresh selling. Cut stems just before flower opens completely.

BEST VARIETIES FOR CUTTING
Any named varieties in your area. Come in orange, scarlet, white, pink, lavender, etc. All lush.

DRYING
Pods good for drying.

❀ *Penstemon*

(Beard Tongue)   Zones 3–10
Many varieities but only a few for cutting. Slim, bell-like flowers in pinks and reds on tall stems.

CULTURE
Prefer good drainage, cool summers, and no fertilizer.

PROPAGATION
Seed or nursery starts.

HARVEST AND CONDITIONING
Cut when flowers first open. Use warm water and preservative. Only last a few days.

BEST VARIETIES FOR CUTTING
P. barbatus. P. gloxinoides for zones 9–10.

DRYING
Not recommended.

❀ *Phlox*   Zones 3–9

Large heads of showy, bright, fragrant flowers on tall stems.

CULTURE
Needs deep, enriched, porous soil and lots of water. But don't wet foliage.

PROPAGATION
Spring divisions. Tip cuttings in summer.

HARVEST AND CONDITIONING
Cut when flower clusters are 1/4 to 1/2 open. Split stems and condition in cold water for several hours.

BEST VARIETIES FOR CUTTING
P. paniculata, plus any hybrid varieties available in your area.

DRYING
Not recommended.

❀ *Physostegia*

(False Dragonhead. Obedient Plant)   Zones 3–10
Long spikes of handsome white, pink, or rose colored flowers. Blooms late in season.

CULTURE
Easily grown in wet or dry soils. Likes full sun. Can be invasive.

PROPAGATION
Seeds or spring divisions.

HARVEST AND CONDITIONING
Cut when flower stalk is 1/2 open. Use warm water and preservative.

BEST VARIETIES FOR CUTTING
P. virginiana .

DRYING
Not recommended.

❀ *Platycodon*

(Balloon Flower)   Zones 3–10

Platycodon (Balloon flower)

Bud looks like a balloon, the flower is star shaped and quite pretty.

CULTURE
Likes full sun but not being moved. Slow to return in the spring.

PROPAGATION
Seeds are tricky. Buy starts.

HARVEST AND CONDITIONING
Cut when one or two flowers on stem are just open. Large buds will open in water, tight ones will not. Sear stems immediately with flame or boiling water.

BEST VARIETIES FOR CUTTING
Try any named variety available in your area.

DRYING
Not recommended

❁ *Polemonium*

(Jacob's Ladder)   Zones 3–9
Dainty blue and white flower stems with attractive leaves.

CULTURE
Likes cool, slightly shady and moist conditions.

PROPAGATION
Seeds, spring or fall divisions, or summer cuttings.

HARVEST AND CONDITIONING
Cut when flowers first open. Use warm water and preservative.

BEST VARIETIES FOR CUTTING
P. caeruleum. P. foliosissimum.

DRYING
Not recommended.

❁ *Rudbeckia*

(Coneflower)   Zones 3–10
Golden yellow petals with blackish cones. Long blooming, tall; great in the garden and as a cut flower.

CULTURE
Easily grown in full sun or light shade.

PROPAGATION
Seeds or spring divisions.

HARVEST AND CONDITIONING
Cut when flowers are first open and centers are tight. Leave overnight in water if possible.

BEST VARIETIES FOR CUTTING
R. fulgida.

DRYING
Flowers can be dried in silica, or flower centers air dried.

❁ *Salvia*

(Sage)   Zones 4–10
Many varieties, both perennial and annual. Many have

fine flowers for cutting, some are fragrant. Usually have small flowers with grey, often woolly foliage.

CULTURE
Easily grown. Need sun.

PROPAGATION
Seeds, spring divisions, and summer stem cuttings. All easy.

HARVEST AND CONDITIONING
Cut when flowers on a stem are 1/2 open. Use warm water and preservative. If odor is too strong, use a little bleach in the water.

BEST VARIETIES FOR CUTTING
S. azurea, S. x superba, S. coccinea, or try any nursery variety not sold as an herb. Also, try clary sage as an annual.

DRYING
Best variety is *Salvia farinacea,* Blue Bedder.

❀ *Scabiosa*

(Pincushion Flower)   Zones 3–10

A frilly border of petals around the "pincushion" center. Also available as an annual.

CULTURE
Needs well drained, sunny location and lots of water in the summer. May need staking.

PROPAGATION
Try to get very fresh seed. Can be divided in spring or fall.

Scabiosa
(Pincushion flower)

HARVEST AND CONDITIONING
Cut when flower is half open, remove leaves, treat with warm water and preservative.

BEST VARIETIES FOR CUTTING
S. caucasica.

DRYING
Pick and air dry centers after petals fall.

❀ *Stokesia*

(Stokes' Aster)   Zones 5–10

Unusual blue aster-like blossom, 2 to 4 inches across.

CULTURE
Sun or light shade. Needs good drainage.

PROPAGATION
Seeds, spring divisions, or root cuttings.

HARVEST AND CONDITIONING
Cut when flowers first open. Strip stems. Use warm water and preservative.

BEST VARIETIES FOR CUTTING
S. laevis. Many named cultivars.

DRYING
Not recommended.

❀ *Thalictrum*
(Meadow Rue)   Zones 5–10
Tall ferny foliage topped by delicate sprays of usually purple flowers. Ideal for bouquets.

CULTURE
Likes partial shade and not being moved. Otherwise, easily grown.

PROPAGATION
Seeds or spring divisions.

HARVEST AND CONDITIONING
Cut when flower sprig is half open. Use warm water and preservative.

BEST VARIETIES FOR CUTTING
T. aquilegifolium, T. delavayi (for hot climates.)

DRYING
Air dry flowers or the seed clusters that form.

❀ *Trollius*
(Globeflower)   Zones 3–10
Buttercup yellow to orange globes on tall stems. Flowers resemble ranunculus.

CULTURE
Originally a bog plant, so give it moist soil and light shade.

PROPAGATION
Needs very fresh seed to sow. Fall divisions.

HARVEST AND CONDITIONING
Cut as buds, half open or fully open. All are attractive. Use warm water and preservative. Leave several hours in cooler, if possible.

BEST VARIETIES FOR CUTTING
T. cultorum, T. eurpeus, T. ledebourii, or try any available in your area.

DRYING
Not recommended.

❀ *Veronica*
(Speedwell)   Zones 4–9
Tall spikes of tiny true blue flowers on small shrub-like plant.

CULTURE
Easy to grow on average well drained soil.

PROPAGATION
Seeds, cuttings, divisions.

HARVEST AND CONDITIONING
Cut when stems are half in flower. Use warm water, preservative.

BEST VARIETIES FOR CUTTING
V. gentianoides, V. grandis holophylla, V. longifolia.

DRYING
Air dry or in silica.

EXPERTS' CHOICE
PERENNIALS

ACANTHUS	Bear's breech
AGAPANTHUS	Lily of the Nile
ANTHURIUM	
ASCLEPIAS	Milkweed
BAPTISIA australis	False Indigo
BELLIS perennis	English Daisy
BOLTONIA	
ERIGERON	Fleabane
EUSTOMA (*Lisianthus*)	Prairie Gentian
FREESIA	
GERBERA jamesonii	Transvaal Daisy
HELICONIA	Lobster Claw
HELLEBORUS niger	Chrstmas Rose
HESPERIS matronalis	Dame's Rocket
LINUM	Flax
LOBELIA cardinalis	Hardy Lobelia
L. siphilitica	
MACLEAYA cordata	Plume poppy
MERTENSIA virginica	Virginia-Bluebells
OENOTHERA	Evening Primrose
ORCHID	
PHYSALIS alkekengi	Chinese Lantern Plant
PRIMULA	
RANUNCULUS	

SAPONARIA	Soapwort
SOLIDAGO	Golden Rod
STRELITZIA	Bird of Paradise
THERMOPSIS	False Lupine
TRADESCANTIA	Spiderwort
VERBASCUM	Mullein

AUTHOR'S CHOICE
ANNUALS AND BIENNIALS

The perennials you grow can provide many unusual plants for much of the year in your garden, flowers not often seen in flower shops, flowers that can earn you good money. But when it comes to mid-summer, your primary harvest then will no doubt come from the annuals and biennials you grow.

Annuals are the easily grown plants that germinate and grow quickly, producing full flowers within the very first growing season or, in the case of biennials, early the second season. Annuals will also fill out your garden and planting areas during the first year or so before your perennials begin full production.

Perennials, as you probably already know, are plants that usually only produce greenery the first year and whose roots then remain alive in the ground to reproduce greenery and flowers season after season.

Some species of plants actually have varieties that are listed as annuals and varieties that are listed as perennials. As a matter of fact, sometimes perennials will act much more like an annual or a biennial.

Furthermore, some lists of flowers seem to confuse

the types and you occasionally will find a plant listed as an annual or biennial in one place and as a perennial in another. I have seen the same variety of Campanula or Canterbury Bells, for instance, listed as a perennial in one seed catalog and as an annual or biennial in another. Not to worry. If it's a plant you want, try growing it and see how it behaves in your ground. Let the botanists argue the finer details.

Another big advantage many annuals have is a fairly long blooming time and a "cut and come again" quality that gives more blossoms the more you harvest them—all fine attributes in flowers for selling.

Annuals are also very inexpensive if grown from seed and can be relatively inexpensive when purchased in six-pacs. Just be certain the label lists the height of the variety you are buying when you do buy starts, as there are so many hybrids these days and many of them are grown as dwarf plants for border edgings or window boxes. A careful reading of the plant label will tell you what you can expect in plant size and stem height. I wouldn't buy any plant for flower cutting that described the stem height as less than fifteen inches.

The following annuals are my favorites for a cut flower garden. I have added notes on anything unusual in their growing habits or harvest and conditioning needs. More annuals are listed in the Experts' Choice list and in the list of Flowers for Drying.

ALTHAEA rosea Hollyhock. Usually sold as a biennial, but annual varieties are now available in seeds and starts. Needs full sun. Cut when 3 or 4 flowers on a stem are open. Fill and plug stems and sear stem end in flame or boiling water. Place in warm water with preservative.

ANTIRRHINUM Snapdragon. Grown as a perennial in zones 9 & 10. Available in many heights and even more colors. Needs full sun. Cut stems when half in flower. Use warm water and preservative.

CALENDULA **Pot Marigold.** Oh so easy to grow and use. Good through fall and even through mild winters. Re-seeds easily. Needs sun. Cut when flowers are 3/4 open. Remove all bottom foliage. Use warm water and preservative.

CALLISTEPHUS chinensis China Asters. Many varieties, many colors. Almost all are long lasting, fine bouquet flowers. Cut when 3/4 to fully open. Use warm water and preservative.

CELOSIA **Cockscomb.** Plume and comb varieties make unusual floral additions. Relatively slow growing, so start indoors early. Needs sun. Cut plume varieties when at least 3/4 developed. Cut comb types when they are full color and the size you want. Strip stems, set in warm water with preservative. Good for drying.

CENTAUREA **Bachelor's Button.** Cornflower. Blue, blue, blue so welcome in bouquets and in the garden. Blooms best in cool weather. Cut when flowers are first open. Use warm water and preservative. Can be dried.

CHRYSANTHEMUM **Annual Chrysanthemums** are daisy-like, easily grown plants that are sold as *C. carinatum,* or *C. coronarium.* All grow best in full sun. Strip all leaves below the water line, put in warm water and preservatives.

CLARKIA Sow seeds where you want them to grow. Dry soil O.K. Needs full sun. Does well in cool weather. Cut stems when three or four flowers are open. Split stems. Put in warm water with preservative.

CLEOME **Spider Flower.** Scented, airy flowers.

These do best in warm weather. Stems have thorns. Cut when clusters are 1/2 open. Use preservative and warm water.

COSMOS Popular tender annual. Taller ones may require staking. Cut when flowers first open and centers are still very tight. Put in deep cold water almost up to the flower head for several hours or overnight.

DAHLIA Many varieties can be grown from seed as an annual, but these may be slow to bloom, and the truest colors come from those grown from tubers. (See Bulb, Corm, & Tuber listing.) Choose dahlia seed varieties that promise at least 15 to 20 inches of height. Cut dahlias when flowers have just opened, sear the stem ends, strip the leaves below the water line and place in warm water and preservative.

DIANTHUS barbatus Sweet William. Excellent colorful and fragrant flower stems in white, pink, reds and varicolored. Biennials that easily reseed themselves. When clusters are 1/2 open, cut just above the stem joints. Use warm water and preservative.

DIGITALIS Foxglove. Medicinal plant that is also poisonous, but quite beautiful. Ample tube flowers often have speckles in the throat. Cut when barely half the blossoms are open, fill stem with water, plug, and set in warm water and preservative.

GOMPHRENA Globe amaranth. Thick clover-like heads in nice colors. Likes warm weather. Cut when flowers are nearly open. Split stems, use warm water and preservative. Dries well.

GYPSOPHILA elegans Annual baby's breath. Short lived, but very attractive filler plant. Cut sprays when half of the flowers are open. Use warm water and preservative. Dries well.

HELIANTHUS Sunflower. Smaller variety, *H.*

debilis, is best for cut flowers. Easily grown. Strip stem bottoms, use warm water and preservative. If heads are too heavy, use florist wire inserted in stem to make them hold up.

HELICHRYSUM Strawflower. Easily grown, straw-like daisy used in fresh bouquets and as a popular dried flower. Cut when flowers have just opened. Use warm water and preservative.

LARKSPUR Annual variety of delphinium. Excellent as cut flower and for drying. Needs a very early start in spring. Use warm water and preservative.

LATHYRUS odoratus Sweet Pea. In great demand as cut flowers. Find varieties with extra long stems. Cut when first two blossoms on a stem are open. Use warm water and preservative.

LIMONIUM sinuatum Annual Statice. Desirable fresh or dried cut flower. Easily grown in sun. Many nice shades. For fresh, cut when flowers have barely opened, place in warm water with preservative.

LUNARIA Honesty or Money Plant. Lightly fragrant filler flower sometimes found in the wild. Cut when first opened. Use warm water and preservative. Also nice for dried seed pods.

MATHIOLA Annual Stock. Fragrant, colorful flower stems. Seeds a little tricky to germinate. Needs 50° temperature. Cut when stems are 1/4 open, split stems if they need it. Remove all leaves below water line, and use preservative and *cold* water.

NEMESIA strumosa Prefers cool weather, but needs sun. Cut when flowers first open and put in warm water and preservative.

NICOTIANA Flowering Tobacco. Nicely scented, likes semi-shade. Sometimes self-seeds. Cut when half of flowers in a cluster are open. Use warm water and preservative.

NIGELLA damascena **Love-In-A-Mist.** Fine as fresh cut flower or dried seed pod. Easily grown. Sometimes self-seeds. Cut when flower first opens and use warm water and preservative.

PAPAVER rhoeas **Shirley Poppy.** Crepe-like petals in wonderful colors. Sow seeds out of doors in fall or spring. Cut when buds show full color. Burn stem ends and place in cold deep water up to flower heads.

PHLOX drummondii **Annual Phlox.** Easily grown from seeds in ground after frost, or start indoors early. Prefers cool weather. Cut when 1/2 open. Use preservative and cold water. Cut stems just above joints.

SALPIGLOSSIS sinuata **Painted Tongue.** Unusual colors in small funnel-shaped blossoms. Do not cover seeds. Harvest when blossoms first open. Remove greens. Put in cold water up to flower heads for several hours.

SCABIOSA atropurpurea **Sweet Scabious.** Can be very tall. Perennial variety also good for cut flowers. Cut when flowers are almost fully open. Split stems. Use warm water and preservative.

SCHIZANTHUS **Butterfly Flower.** Very tender annuals, sensitive to both heat and cold. Small orchid-like flowers in nice colors. Split stems and burn with a flame or boiling water. Use preservative and warm water.

TAGETES **Marigolds.** Many varieties in seeds and starts. Buy only tallest varieties. Cut when petals open but centers are still tight. Use warm water and preservative.

ZINNIA Excellent cut flower in many colors. Cut when blossoms are fully open but centers still very tight. Use preservative and warm water.

EXPERTS' CHOICE
ANNUALS AND BIENNIALS

AGERATUM	Flossflower
AGROSTEMMA githago	Corn Cockle
AMBROSINIA mexicana	Jerusalem Oak
AMMI majus	Queen Anne's Lace
AMMOBIUM alatum	Winged Everlasting
BUPLEURUM rotundifolium	
CARTHAMUS tinctorius	False Saffron
CHEIRANTHUS	Wallflower
COLEUS	
CYNOGLOSSUM amabile	Chinese Forget-me-not
DIMORPHOTHECA aurantiaca	Cape-Marigold
ECHIUM plantaginea	
EMILIA javanica	Tassel Flower
EUPHORBIA marginata	Snow-On-The-Mountain
GILIA	Queen Anne's Thimble
GODETIA	
HELIOTROPIUM	Heliotrope
HELIPTERUM roseum	Strawflower
IBERIS	Candytuft
LAVATERA trimestris	Annual Mallow
LAYIA	Tidy Tips
LEPTOSYNE	
LINARIA	Toadflax
LOBULARIA	Sweet Alyssum
MALOPE	Mallow

MOLUCCELLA laevis	Bells of Ireland
NEMESIA strumosa	
NICANDRA	
PAPAVER nudicaule	Iceland Poppy
PAPAVER somniferum	Opium Poppy
PETUNIA	
RESEDA odorata	Mignonette
TRACHELIUM	Blue Throatwort
VERBENA	

AUTHOR'S CHOICE
TREES, VINES, AND SHRUBS

It doesn't take long to figure out that some of the most handsome and even dramatic cut flowers can come from the most basic plants in our gardens: the shrubs, vines, and even the trees that seldom need much care and add so much to our landscaping.

Many shrubs and trees need annual pruning and it's often easy to make the pruning fit in with the cut flower supply—trimming and shaping your trees, shrubs, and vines as you take the cut branches to market. But it is important to have a good shrub and tree gardening guide or two on hand when you decide to trim and prune your shrubs, because you can affect the plants very much by what you do and when you do it.

Following are the shrubs and trees I have used in my bouquets. The Experts' Choice list that follows is even longer.

Almost all of these plants have woody stems of one kind or another. So be certain to split the stems when needed, strip the bark if necessary, and keep an eye during conditioning. If you see the leaves of branches start to wilt, put them in fresh, very warm water again, or even submerge the whole stem or branch in water. There's quite a lot of material that needs hydrating in tree or shrub stems. Make sure they get plenty of water taken up in their cells before you take them to market or they may wilt.

ABELIA grandiflora. Prefers sun or light shade. White or pinkish flowers, summer to fall. Easily grown. Flowers appear on new growth. Warm water and preservative.

AZALEA. Needs acid soil, lots of moisture, and good drainage. Fine cut flowers in many colors. Cut when half the flowers in a cluster are open. Be certain to split stems before conditioning. Use preservative and cold water.

BERBERIS Barberry. Easily grown. Good greenery and flowers in several varieties. Cut off spines for use in arrangements. Use warm water and preservatives.

BUDDLEIA. Fragrant summer flowers on tall arching branches. Cut when flower spike is 1/2 open. Use warm or even hot water to condition, and allow several hours.

CHAENOMELES Japanese Quince. Very early spring buds which can be forced into early blooming. Or wait and cut branches when flowers are 1/4 open on a stem. Remove any thorns. Warm water and preservative.

CORNUS florida Flowering Dogwood. Budding branches can be forced and greenery adds interest to bouquets. Split stems and use warm water and preservative.

COTINUS coggygria Smoke Tree. Very attractive branches and tiny flowers. Var. *purpureus* is especially colorful and worth having. Use warm water and preservative.

COTONEASTER. Many varieties, easily grown. Useable flowers, fruits, buds, even fall colors in leaves. Use warm water and preservative.

CRATAEGUS **Hawthorn Tree**. Wonderful spring buds and blossoms from white to pink to scarlet. Also useable branches of berries in the fall. Very sharp thorns need removing. Warm or hot water and preservative.

CYTISUS **Broom**. Domestic and wild varieties good for both bloom and arching stems of greenery. Use warm water and preservative. Flowers are pea-like.

EUONYMUS. Many species, most of which have fine foliage. *E. alata* is quite lovely, turning dark red in the fall. Flowers are not very showy. Warm water and preservative.

FORSYTHIA. One of the earliest bloomers, and endless greenery until winter. Can be forced to bloom very, very early. Yellow flower clusters signify spring. Use warm water and preservatives.

HEDERA **Ivy**. The perfect greenery for many uses. Soak stems in cold water (submerged) for a couple of hours to clean and condition. Always cut just above the stem node.

HYDRANGEA. Cut when barely half the cluster is open. Split stems, boil or sear with flame for 20 seconds or so. Also good for drying. Needs acid soil for blue flowers.

HYPERICUM **St. Johnswort**. From ground covers to small shrubs. Bright yellow flowers last a long time if cut when flowers are fully open and stems are split. Use warm water and preservative.

ILEX **Holly**. Useful, very dark, glossy greenery. Slow growing, so be careful about over pruning. Best to take from very large shrubs. Split stems, use warm water and preservative.

KALMIA latifolia Mountain Laurel. Good foliage plus pink flower clusters that are long lasting. Can be pruned any time of the year. Split stems. Use warm water and preservative.

KOLKWITZIA Beauty Bush. Buds for forcing, plus pink sprays of flowers and atttractive foliage. Split stems. Use warm water and preservative.

LABURNUM Golden Chaintree. Drooping clusters of yellow flowers. Cut when cluster is only half open. Split stems and condition overnight.

LONICERA Honeysuckle. Many showy varieties that can be cut and used in arrangements. Easily grown. Split stems and use warm water.

MAGNOLIA soulangeana. Can be forced to bloom inside, or cut when flowers first open. Other varieties available are useful for cut flowers also. Split woody stems and condition in warm water.

MAHONIA aquifolium Oregon Grape or Holly. Easily grown or collected in the wild in some areas. Yellow flowers, blue berries, dark, glossy foliage. Many uses. Lasts a long time with minimum conditioning.

MALUS Flowering Crab-Apple. Lovely flowers that can be forced in early spring, or cut and used when in blossom. Split stems, use warm water.

PHILADELPHUS Mock Orange. Fragrant white flower clusters. Prune by cutting for bouquets. Flowers only come on second year's growth. Split stems, use warm water.

PRUNUS Flowering Almond, Apricot, Cherries, Peach, Plum, etc. Can be cut very early spring for forcing, or when first breaking flower. See the section on forcing flowering branches in the Harvest and Conditioning chapter.

PYRACANTHA. Can be used when in flower as a

filler or greenery; also good in the fall with red berries, which can be sprayed with clear plastic to make them last longer. Split stems, use warm water.

RHODODENDRON. Fabulous selection of flower colors. Cut when barely half a flower cluster is open. These do best in acid soils. Split stems, use warm water and preservative.

ROSES. Almost every type of rose can be used in bouquets. Be sure to split the stems well, and put in warm water with preservative and then condition overnight, if possible, in deep water in your cooler or refrigerator. Remove thorns and bottom leaves. Recommended cultivars for cutting include: Red, Olympiad; White, Pascali; Pink, Bewitched; Yellow, Gold Medal. But almost any rose of almost any type goes well in bouquets.

SALIX Willow. Very useful in several forms. Earliest budding branches of *S. caprea* can make excellent bouquets or can even be sold separately. Branches of *S. matsudana Tortuosa* are also excellent in bouquets, with or without foliage. *S. sachalinensis Sekka* is another willow much used by florists and flower arrangers.

SPIREA. Excellent plant for arrangers. Comes in different varieties, almost all have fine flowers, and are easily grown. Split any woody stems and put in warm water.

SYRINGA Lilac. Everyone's favorite. Cut when clusters are only 1/4 to 1/2 open. Remove foliage to make flowers last longer. Takes several hours to condition.

TAMARIX Tamarisk. **Pink Cascade.** Unusual, plumy pink flowers and nice foliage. One of my personal favorites. Flowers and foliage both useful. Split stems and use warm water and preservative.

VIBURNUM. V. burkwoodi, V. tomentosum, V. opulus, V. fragrans, V. carlesi and others. Popular, easy to grow shrubs that produce graceful white flowers and handsome foliage. Split any woody stems and put in warm water with preservative.

WISTERIA. Fragrant flower clusters that can be used in bouquets. Cut when first flowers open, split stems and treat with warm water and preservative. Can also be hung to dry, or forced to bloom early.

EXPERTS' CHOICE
TREES, VINES & SHRUBS

There are so many worthwhile plants to choose from in this list that it only makes me wish I had more room to plant. Flowering shrubs, trees, and vines are surely the easiest of plants to take care of, the nicest of plants we can add to our landscaping. That they also can produce harvestable, saleable flowers is rather amazing.

ACACIA	
ACER	Japanese Maple
ALBIZZIA	Hardy Silk Tree
CALLUNA	Scotch Heather
CALYCANTHUS	Sweetshrub or
	Carolina Allspice
CAMELLIA JAPONICA	Camellia
CARYOPTERIS	Blue Spirea
CERCIS canadensis	Redbud
CHAMAELAUCIUM uncinatum	Waxflower
CHIONANTHUS virginicus	Fringe Tree
CLEMATIS	
DEUTZIA	
ELEAGNUS angustifolia	Russian Olive
ENKIANTHUS campanulatus	
ERICA	Heather
EUCALYPTUS	
FUCHSIA	Hardy varieties
GARDENIA jasminoides	
HAMAMELIS	Witch Hazel

HIBISCUS syriacus	Althea or Rose of Sharon
KERRIA japonica	Kerrybush
LEPTOSPERMUM	Tea Tree
LEUCOSPERMUM	
LEUCOTHOE fontanesiana	Drooping Leucothoe
LINDERA benzoin	Spicebush
MYRTUS	Myrtle
NEILLIA thibetica	
OXYDENDRUM arboreum	Sour Wood Tree
POTENTILLA fruticosa	Buttercup Shrub
PROTEA	
STEPHANOTIS	
STEWARTIA ovata	
SYMPHORICARPOS	Snowberry
VACCINIUM corymbosum	Highbush Blueberry
VITEX	Chaste Tree

AUTHOR'S CHOICE
BULBS, CORMS, TUBERS, ETC.

ALLIUM Flowering Onions. We all love the edibles in this genus (there are over 400 species in all) but the ornamental onions offer some wondrous flowers for cutting. Many can be grown from seed, but will take much longer to produce flowers. They all should be picked when about half of the florets have opened, placed in warm water with preservative and, if the smell is a little unpleasant, add a tablespoon of bleach to the water to control the odor. Almost all the alliums may be dried successfully. See the Herbs section for other allium choices.

Best varieties for cutting: *A. aflatunense, A. christophi, A. giganteum, A. histafolium, A. pulchellium, A. oreophilum, A. siculum, A. spherocephalum.*

CROCOSMIA masoniorum. Sometimes called common montbretia. A very showy plant of red-orange that blooms in late summer and makes a fine cut flower. Lucifer Crocosmia is also an excellent variety. Does best in full sun. Cut when 1/3 of the flowers are open, put in warm water with preservative.

DAHLIA. The loveliest, most colorful dahlias are

available from tubers, either from a nursery, mail order supplier, or handed across a backyard fence by a good neighbor gardener. If you grow them as an annual from seed (see the annual listing) and get colors and sizes you like, these can be dug up before frost and grown as a tuber the following years. In other words, dahlias come true from tubers, but not always true from seed. They need lots of sun and a rich, well fertilized soil. In cold climates, they must be dug up and stored over winter. Huge dinner plate size dahlias are not very good for bouquets or florist use; 3 to 5 inch blossoms are probably the best for commercial use. Some of the nicest types to grow are the waterlily dahlias, the smaller cactus dahlias, spider dahlias, and the pompon dahlias. Harvest when the flowers are just fully opened, strip the stems of any leaves that would be in water, sear the stems and put in warm water and preservative.

GLADIOLUS. Lots of fans for this one. The largest ones are not as easy to use in arrangements as the medium and smaller sizes. The size of the stem and flower are completely related to the size of the corm. The small *nanus* variety is often grown as a perennial, and is particularly nice to grow for bouquets. Medium and larger varieties are easily sold by the stem.

Glad corms or bulbs are available quite inexpensively and, with care, can last for quite a few years. Cut when the second blossom on the stem has opened. They are the one flower that can be cut during the middle of the day, and then left out of the water for at least a half an hour. This delays the bud opening. Be sure to leave as much greenery as possible on the plant when you cut if you plan to dig up the bulbs in fall for replanting in the spring. Split stems and leave the glads at room temperature in cool water with preservative for several hours.

Water high in fluoride content can damage glads.

IRIS. A true workhorse for the florist industry and one of the finest of garden flowers, too. Three types are especially good for cutting. Dutch iris, which come in several outstanding colors and can be planted either in spring or fall; Siberian iris, handsome graceful blossoms on tall stems with equally tall grassy foliage; and Tall bearded iris which are quite dramatic and beautiful, in colors ranging from white to almost black. The Dutch iris grow from bulbs, the other two types from rhizomes. All are relatively easy to grow, all make excellent additions to bouquets. Cut all iris when the buds show full color or (for bearded iris) when the first blossom just begins to open. The flower petals are fragile and the earlier picked the better they are. Use preservative, put in cool water and leave at room temperature until used.

LILIUM Lilies. Watch out, flower lovers and gardeners, these can become addictive! They come into flower just after all the spring perennials, and, if different types are planted, can bloom all summer long. Many are fragrant (a few of them almost overwhelmingly so) and come in several different forms such as trumpet or saucer shaped, upward or outward facing, and some whose petals curve backwards completely. Lily hybridizers are a busy bunch and offer new strains every year without fail. Care must be taken in cutting lilies in order to protect the plants. It is preferable not to cut the lily flower the first year of bloom, and then to cut it only every other year. When cutting, take only the top 1/3 to 1/2 of the stem, leaving as much of the greenery as possible to nourish the bulb for the following year. Split the stems, put in warm water with preservative. The pollen on the flower anthers should be removed before taking lilies to market, as it can smudge up clothing and furniture. Many types of lilies are good for cut flowers, but the outward or upward facing ones are probably the best. I urge you to try some lilies. You will never be sorry. They are perfect for bouquets, florists want to buy them all the time, and nowadays there's a large trade in potted lilies of many kinds (besides the popular Easter lily, *L. longiflorium*).

NARCISSUS Daffodil. The earliest of cut flowers and sometimes the very best, so welcome after a long, colorless winter. There are many varieties, some of them too short to be of use for cutting. Grow only those promising 14" or more. Be sure to try some of the multi-flowered types such as Cheerfulness and Thalia. Daffodils are best cut at what is called the "gooseneck" stage, when the full bud color is showing but it has not opened at all. Cut the stem as long as possible, yet remove as little of the foliage as possible. That must feed the bulb for next year's blossom. Place daffodils in a bucket by themselves for at least an hour or so. The sap they produce may harm other flowers. If you have to recut them, put them alone again for an hour or so. Preservative is not necessary for daffodils. They can also be held safely out of water at low temperatures (35°-40°) for several days.

SCILLA CAMPANULATA Blue wood hyacinth. Almost too short, but so long lasting and helpful in spring bouquets that they are worth it. Besides, they add so much to the garden and are especially easy to grow.

TULIPA Tulip. Since the "Tulip Craze" of the 17th century, we've all been a little nutsy over tulips. The Dutch (primarily) have developed so many varieties and strains through history that now there are thick catalogs with seemingly endless choices in colors and types, from single early tulips to double late tulips, from fringed tulips to lily-flowered tulips, from little 8" high varieties to 30" show stoppers. Tulips are easily grown in all but the driest and warmest of climates, but most recommend that they be dug up in June or July and held over until fall for re-planting. Actually, the first-year tulip flowers from a bulb are the best, although some decent flowers may bloom for several years after, whether they are dug up and replanted or not. Cut the tulips when the full bud color shows, split the stems and place in cold water in a narrow bucket. Wrap paper around the top of the bucket so that the buds and flowers will not bend over too far. Keep them that way until ready to take to market. Commercial tulip bunches are kept in very cold, dry storage for days, even weeks, wrapped in cellophane to keep them snug and protected.

EXPERTS' CHOICE
BULBS, CORMS, TUBERS, ETC.

ACIDANTHERA	
ANEMONE coronaria	
CANNA	
FREESIA	
FRITILLARIA	
HIPPEASTRUM	Amaryllis
ISMENE	Spider Lily
IXIA	African Corn Lily
LEUCOJUM	Snowflake
NERINE bowdenii	
ORNITHOGALUM thyrsoides	Chincherinchee
POLIANTHES tuberosa	Tuberose
RANUNCULUS	
SPARAXIS	Harlequin flower
TRITONIA	Montbretia
WATSONIA	

HERBS AS CUT FLOWERS

These are the herbs I would recommend that you consider growing as possible greenery for bouquets, as flowers in their own right, or as nice fragrant touches to bouquets you put together.

Herbs are easily grown in almost any kind of soil or weather conditions and they are very useful in the kitchen and around the house. Many are also very good for decorative drying. Condition them all with warm water and preservative after cutting.

ANGELICA. A biennial herb that self-sows readily. Fragrant leaves and flowers. Hollow stems that need filling and plugging if used in a bouquet.

ARTEMISIAS. A large group of plants that includes both French tarragon and dusty miller. Most have very interesting grey-green foliage which is easily used in arrangements. Recommended varieties include *A. albula, A. lactiflora,* and *A. stelleriana.*

CHIVES *Allium schoenoprasum.* One of the nicest of bouquet flowers, small magenta blossoms that last a long time. Easily grown. Divide every couple of years.

COSTMARY *Chrysanthemum balsamita.* The very pleasing aroma of balsam, plus soft, slightly furry leaves (often pressed for book marks), and yellow button flowers. Can be a invasive, but quite nice.

DILL *Anethum graveolens.* Buy the tall, standard version of dill, not the little ferny one that is grown only for culinary use. The tall type is the one grown for pickle making and also makes rather handsome additions to flower bouquets. Easily grown in the sun.

FENNEL *Foeniculum vulgare.* Tall ferny stems in green or bronze that make fine greenery.

HYSSOP *Hyssopus officinalis.* The perfect bee feeding plant, hyssop also adds color and greenery to bouquets. The odor is strong for some people.

LAVENDER. Look for the tallest varieties available, grow all you can, and enjoy. Long lasting, great for drying, too, and loved by all.

LEMON BALM *Melissa officinalis.* Another fine greenery plant with a delightful aroma. Lends itself to informal bouquets; some people even think of it as weedy.

LEMON VERBENA *Aloysia triphylla.* A personal favorite because the leaves are so aromatic. It is not winter hardy, but cuttings are easily taken.

MINT *Mentha.* Peppermints and apple mints are probably the best to try for greenery as they usually grow tall and produce lots of flowers. But peppermint is not available from seed, so start with nursery stock or cuttings from a friend.

MONARDA Bee balm. Tall, attractive garden plant with unusual, long lasting flowers that bees and hummingbirds visit often. Cut when only 1/4 of the blooms are open. Remove bottom leaves.

RUE *Ruta graveolens.* Blue-green lacy foliage with small dainty yellow flowers. Quite a nice cut flower garden addition.

SALVIAS. These are covered in the annual list, but I put them here again just to remind readers that there are many wonderful varieties of sage plants and flowers to try. Try them.

SWEET CICELY *Myrrhis odorata.* Ferny, lacy leaves with white flowers and a nice fragrance. Only freshest seed will germinate. Start with nursery stock.

FLOWERS FOR DRYING

My own experience in drying flowers is pitifully poor. I have a fine screen my husband built that hangs from the ceiling above the wood stove and, when I remember, I fill it with summer rose petals that make the house fragrant as we start the fall wood burning. But I don't always remember and sometimes they are there for a couple of years without my even noticing.

I have dried herbs and strawflowers, statice and Chinese lanterns from the ceiling of my basement and then wondered what to do with them. I usually just give them away to friends who seem to be much more talented in such crafts. But over the years, I have noticed a strong connection between fresh flower growers and dried flower enthusiasts—often they are the very same people.

So, for the benefit of all the fresh flower growers with a yearning to try their hand with a few of the "drieds," following is a list I have put together from my own growing, books, and interviews with growers. Most would simply need air drying, but the large and more fragile blossoms would need covering with silica or borax and left to dry for several days or even weeks. See the reference section and bibiliography for books on drying.

ACACIA
ACANTHUS
ACHILLEA
ACROLINIUM
ALBIZIA
ALCHEMILLA mollis
ALLIUM
AMARANTHUS
ANAPHALIS margaritacea
ANEMONE pulsatilla
ANTIRRHINUM
AQUILEGIA
ARMERIA
ARTEMISIA
ASCLEPIAS
ASTER—Michaelmas
  Daisy
ASTILBE
ASTRANTIA
BAPTISIA
BUDDLEIA
CALENDULA
CALLUNA
CALYCANTHUS floridus
CAMPANULA
CANNA
CARTHAMUS tinctorius
CARYOPTERIS
CATANANCHE
CELOSIA
CENTAUREA

CERASTIUM tomentosum
CHRYSANTHEMUM
CINERARIA
CLEMATIS
COLEUS
COREOPSIS
COSMOS
CYTISUS
DAFFODILS
DAHLIA
DAISIES
DAUCUS carota
DELPHINIUM
DEUTZIA
DICENTRA
DICTAMNUS
DIGITALIS
DIPSACUS
ECHINOPS
ERICA
ERYNGIUM
EUPATORIUM
FILIPENDULA
GAILLARDIA
GALTONIA
GILIA capitata
GLADIOLUS
GLOXINIA
GOMPHRENA globosa
GYPSOPHILIA
HELIANTHUS

HELICHRYSUM

HELIPTERUM

HEUCHERA sanguinea

HOSTA

HUMULUS

HYDRANGEA

IBERIS

IRIS

LANTANA

LARKSPUR

LAVANDULA

LEONTOPODIUM

LEUCOTHOE

LIATRIS

LILY

LIMONIUM

LIPPIA citriodora

LIRIOPE

LONAS inodora

LUNARIA

LYTHRUM

MAGNOLIA

MALVA

MARRUBIUM

MATHIOLA incana

MOLUCCELLA

MONARDA

MONTBRETIA

MUSCARI

NARCISSUS

NEPETA

NICANDRA

NIGELLA

ORIGANUM

ORNITHOGALUM

PAEONIA

PAPAVER

PHYSALIS

POLYGONUM

PROTEA

RANUNCULUS

RHUS

ROSA

RUDBECKIA

SALVIA

SEDUM

SILENE

SOLIDAGO

SPIREA

STACHYS.

STRELITZIA

TAGETES

THALICTRUM

TITHONIA

TULIPA

VERBASCUM

VERBENA

VERONICA

XERANTHEMUM

ZINNIA

APPENDIX

ASSOCIATIONS

One of the best ways to continue to get information about growing flowers for sale is to become a member of the Association of Specialty Cut Flower Growers. Once you've decided to grow for a larger market, or for markets outside your own area, these are the people who can offer you special assistance and continuing information on growing and marketing.

They are still quite a small organization, but they have members all over the country who grow what are known in the trade as "minor" or "secondary" cut flower crops—something other than the major crops such as carnations, roses, mums and gladiolus.

That means the organization is looking out for the small growers who are seeking a niche in the flower market. They give conferences every year with interesting speakers and then publish the results economically, so that everyone who couldn't attend the conference knows what went on. They offer plant profiles in every issue of their newsletter and the ads are an interesting way to find out about new techniques and supplies being offered to growers, for instance, where to buy "plugs" which most larger growers now use instead of seeds. Members are also given a membership list so they can keep in touch with other small growers in their area. The Association address is ASCFG, 155 Elm ST., Oberlin, OH 44074. Tel. 216-774-2887. Membership at this time is sixty-five dollars yearly.

REFERENCE MATERIAL

The following books and reference materials may be of help to you in your search for more information about cut flower growing and marketing.

BOOKS

Gardening By Mail, by Barbara J. Barton, Tusker Press, Box 1338, Sebastopol, CA. 95473. An extensive, and yearly updated list of plant and seed sources, horticultural libraries, horticultural societies, professional and trade associations, garden supplies and products, magazines and books pertaining to horticulture.

Ball Culture Guide, by Jim Nau. A basic horticultural growing reference including temperatures for seed germination, spacing in greenhouse or field, staking needs, etc. Available from ASCFG, 155 Elm St., Oberlin, OH 44074. Write for price, which depends on membership.

Herbaceous Perennial Plants, by Allan M. Armitage, Varsity Press, P.O. Box 6301, Athens, GA 30604. Covers most perennials, including those for cutting. Dr. Armitage is one of the leaders in the study of cut-flower production in America.

CATALOGS

Timber Press. 9999 SW Wilshire, Portland, OR 97225. Send for their free catalog of books for gardeners, horticulturists and botanists. They also list books for professional growers.

American Nurseryman Horticulture Books and Videos. 111 No. Canal St. Suite 545, Chicago, IL 60606-7276. Free catalog listing reference books for plants, marketing and merchandising, with the primary emphasis on nurseries. Free.

agAccess. Agricultural Book Catalog. PO Box 2008, Davis, CA 95617. An agricultural information source catalog that includes a section on Floriculture. Free.

Capability's Books. Box 114 Highway 46, Deer Park, WI. 54007. Large, complete garden book catalog featuring many books on individual species. Free.

OTHER

As of this writing, the Association of Specialty Cut Flower Growers is preparing a complete cut flower grower bibliography. Write to them at 155 Elm St., Oberlin, OH 44074.

Write to the National Agricultural Library, Room 111, 10301 Baltimore Blvd., Beltsville, MD 20705 for a list of "Information Products on Horticulture". The list and the publications are free.

Your state agriculture department puts out a market report on flowers, primarily the basics: chrysanthemums, roses, carnations etc.

Flower design shows and design workshops are often staged by large florist supply companies. Ask your local florist or florist supplier to let you know when there will be one in your area. Consider attending for all the good ideas that will be presented.

SEED SOURCES

These are the seed companies that growers have recommended to me, or that I have used and liked myself. I urge you to send for a catalog (most are free) from each of them, and see how their product line suits your particular needs.

Ball Seed Co.
622 Town Road, West Chicago, IL 60185

The Country Garden
PO Box 3539, Oakland, CA 94609-0539
415-658-8777

Harris Seeds
60 Saginaw Drive, PO Box 22960, Rochester, NY
14692-2960
716-442-9386

Johnny's Selected Seeds
Foss Hill Road, Albion, ME 04901
207-437-4301

Modena Seed Co.
5727 Mission St., San Francisco, CA 94112
415-585-2324

Nichols Garden Nursery
1190 North Pacific Highway, Albany, OR 97321-4598
503-967-8406

Norman Seed Co.
7417 Florence Ave., Downey, CA 90240

Park Seed
Cokesbury Road, Greenwood, SC 29647-0001

Pinetree Garden Seeds
New Gloucester, ME 04260
207-926-3400

Shepherd's Garden Seeds
30 Irene St., Torrington, CT 06790
203-482-3638

Stokes
PO Box 548, Buffalo, NY 14240
416-688-4300

Thompson & Morgan Inc.
PO Box 1308, Jackson, NJ 08527
908-363-2225
1-800-274-SEED for orders.

Vaughn's Seeds
5300 Katrine Ave., Downers Grove, IL 60515

BIBLIOGRAPHY

The following books and magazines were helpful in the preparation of this book.

Arranging Cut Flowers, Ortho Books, San Francisco, 1985.

Botany For Gardeners, by Brian Capon, Timber Press, Inc., Portland, Oregon, 1990.

Color Dictionary of Flowers and Plants, by Roy Hack and Patrick M. Synge, Crown Publishers, Inc., New York, 1975.

Complete Book of Cut Flower Care, by Mary Jane Vaughn, Timber Press, Portland, 1988.

Dictionary of Plant Names, by Allen J. Coombes, Timber Press, Portland, Oregon, 1985.

The Dried Flower Book, by Annette Mierhof, E.P. Dutton, New York, 1981.

Everlastings, by Patricia Thorpe, Facts on File Publications, New York, 1985.

The Gardener's Illustrated Encyclopedia of Trees and Shrubs, by Brian Davis, Rodale Press, Emmaus, PA, 1987.

Gardening For Flower Arrangement, by Arno Nehrling and Irene Nehrling, Dover Publications, New York, 1976.

Illustrated Guide To Gardening, Reader's Digest, New York, 1978.

Perennials, How To Select, Grow and Enjoy, by Pamela Harper and Frederick McGourty, HP Books, Tucson, 1985.

Plants From Test Tubes, An Introduction to Micropropagation, by Lydiane Kyte, Timber Press, Portland, 1983.

Postharvest Handling and Storage of Cut Flowers, Florist Greens and Potted Plants, by Joanna Nowak and Ryszard M. Rudnicki, Timber Press, Portland, 1990.

APPENDIX
190

Sunset Western Garden Book, Lane Publishing Co., Menlo Park, CA, 1990.

Taylor's Guide To Shrubs, Houghton Mifflin Co., Boston, 1987.

Taylor's Guide To Bulbs, Houghton Mifflin Co., Boston, 1987.

Taylor's Guide to Annuals, Houghton Mifflin Co., Boston, 1987.

The World of Flower Arranging, by Barbara Pearce, Exeter Books, New York, 1982.

Florist Magazine, An FTD Publication,Southfield, Michigan, April 1991.

Cut Flower Quarterly, Association of Specialty Cut Flower Growers, Inc., Oberlin, Ohio, 1989-1991.

Proceedings of 2nd National Conference on Specialty Cut Flowers, Athens, Georgia, March 1989. Presented by Univ. of Georgia, Dept. of Horticulture. Sponsored by the Association of Specialty Cut Flower Growers, Inc.

INDEX

PLANT INDEX

Abelia grandiflora 163
Acacia 168, 180
Acanthus 152, 180
Acer 33, 168
Achillea (yarrow) 134, 180
Acidanthera 92, 175
Aconitum (monkshood) 92, 134
Acrolinium 105, 180
Aesculus 33
Adenophora 92
Agapanthus 92, 152
Ageratum 92, 160
Agrostemma (corn cockle) 92,
  160
Albizzia (hardy silk tree) 168
Alchemilla mollis (lady's mantle)
  92, 135, 180
Allium 170, 180
Alstroemeria 87, 92, 135
Althaea rosea (hollyhock) 82, 92,
  155
Amaranthus caudatus 92, 180
Amrosinia (Jerusalem oak) 160
Amelanchier canadensis (service-
  berry) 22, 34
Ammi majus 92, 160
Ammobium alatum (winged
  everlaasting) 160
Amsonia 92
Anaphalis margaritacea 180
Anemone, Japanese 93, 135
  A. coronaria 175
  A pulsatilla 180
Angelica 176
Anthurium 152

Antirrhinum (snapdragon) 54,
  71, 73, 75-80, 123, 156
Aquilegia (columbine) 92, 135,
  180
Armeria (thrift) 136, 180
Artemisia 79, 92, 176, 180
Asclepias 152, 180
Asters 92, 136, 180
  China aster 73, 156
  Spider aster 76
Astilbe 92, 137, 180
Astrantia 92, 180
Auctions 114, 119
Azalea 34

baby's breath, see *Gypsophilia*
Baptisia australis (false indigo)
  152, 180
Baronia 113
Bellis perennis 152
Berberis (barberry) 163
bleeding heart, see *Dicentra*
Bletilla 92
Boltonia 152
Buddleia 163
Bupleurum 92, 160
Bupthalmum 92

Calendula (pot marigold) 156,
  180
Callistephus, see *Asters*
Calluna (Scotch heather) 168,
  180
Calycanthus 168, 180
Camellia 168

Lemon Verbena

ORDER FORM

QTY	TITLE	PRICE	TOTAL
	Flowers for Sale: Growing and Marketing Cut Flowers	$14.95	
	Profits from Your Backyard Herb Garden: Growing, Marketing and Packaging Culinary Herbs to Sell to Your Local Grocer or Restaurant	$10.95	
	Subtotal		
	Shipping and Handling (Add $1 for first book; 50¢ for each additional book)		
	Sales Tax (WA residents only add 7%)		
	Total Enclosed		

I understand that I may return any books for a full refund if not satisfied.

YOUR NAME --

ADDRESS ---

CITY ---

STATE ----------------------------------ZIP ---

DAYTIME PHONE ---

Make check payable to and mail to:
SAN JUAN NATURALS
BOX 642S
Friday Harbor, WA 98250

If this is a library book, please photocopy this page.
Thank you for your order!